BAG ... KS II

Phot ... ar and

© DELTA SYSTEMS COMPANY, INC.
1992

LITERACY UNLIMITED

$10.95

ACKNOWLEDGEMENTS

Grateful acknowledgements are due to George Gati for editing and Richard Patchin for his support.

ISBN 0–937354–77–5
First published in 1992 by Delta Systems Co., Inc.
1400 Miller Parkway
McHenry, IL 60050–7030

Printed in the United States of America

Table of Contents

Introduction

- Ever substitute in an ESL class, and the regular teacher didn't leave you a lesson plan?

- Ever find that if the teacher did leave you a lesson plan, it was either illegible, skimpy, or unclear?

- Does your regular ESL textbook need supplementing?

- Need a little help?

If so, BAG OF TRICKS I and II are for you.

The lessons in BAG OF TRICKS I and II are blackline masters designed to be photocopied and distributed to students. Clear, detailed lesson plans accompany each lesson.

BAG OF TRICKS I and II are organized by level of difficulty. It is a collection of lessons that covers a diverse range of topics and key grammatical structures.

- Use the lessons to make overhead transparencies.

- Give them as homework assignments.

- Use them to reinforce your regular lessons.

- Add them to YOUR "bag of tricks."

- Give them to YOUR next substitute!

Beginning
Level

1 Lesson Title

ESL Beginning Level

Directions

1. Study the rules for forming indefinite articles.

Vocabulary

egg	pet
car	box
lamp	pen
man	person
woman	child
orange	door

2. Supply the correct indefinite article. Use the words below.

Spelling Rules

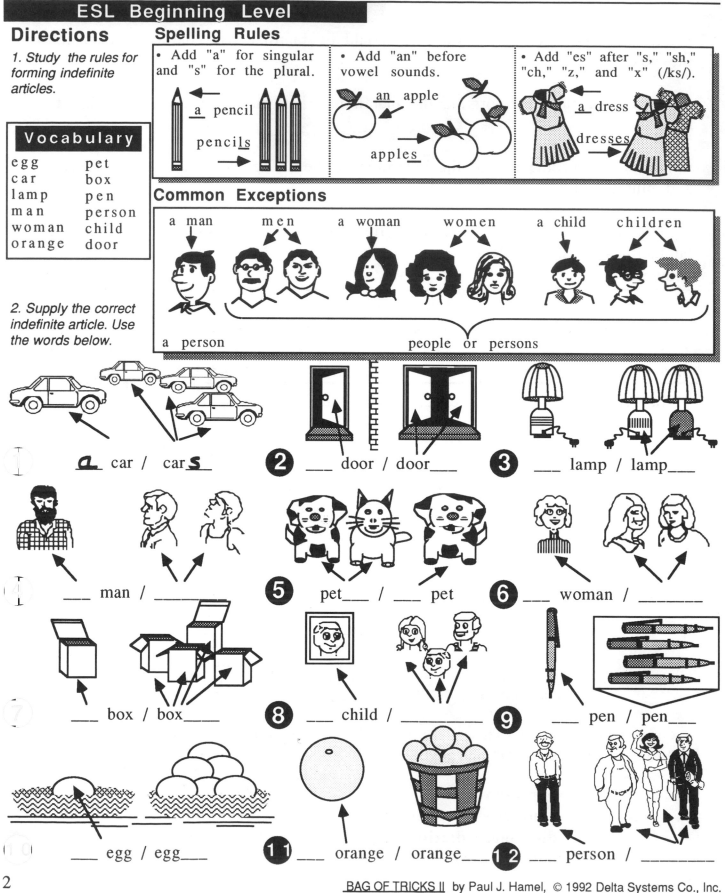

- Add "a" for singular and "s" for the plural.

  <u>a</u> pencil

  pencil<u>s</u>

- Add "an" before vowel sounds.

  <u>an</u> apple

  apple<u>s</u>

- Add "es" after "s," "sh," "ch," "z," and "x" (/ks/).

  <u>a</u> dress

  dress<u>es</u>

Common Exceptions

a man — men — a woman — women — a child — children

a person — people or persons

1. __a__ car / car__s__

2. ___ door / door___

3. ___ lamp / lamp___

4. ___ man / _____

5. pet___ / ___ pet

6. ___ woman / _____

7. ___ box / box___

8. ___ child / _____

9. ___ pen / pen___

10. ___ egg / egg___

11. ___ orange / orange___

12. ___ person / _____

BAG OF TRICKS II by Paul J. Hamel, © 1992 Delta Systems Co., Inc.

1 • Before doing this lesson, students should be familiar with the vocabulary in the box.

• Explain the rules for forming the indefinite article in the boxes at the top of the handout.

• Orally practice the use of the indefinite article. Use pictures to cue singular and plural nouns.

• Next, have the students write the correct article ("a" or "an") or word ending on thelines on the handout.

Answers

1. a car / cars	5. pets / a pet	9. a pen / pens
2. a door / doors	6. a woman / women	10. an egg / eggs
3. a lamp / lamps	7. a box / boxes	11. an orange / oranges
4. a man / men	8. a child / children	12. a person / people

2 • Practice the pronunciation of the plural endings. Tell the students that we pronounce the "s" and "es" three ways :
1. After unvoiced consonants /s/
2. After voiced consonants /z/
3. After /s/, /sh/, /ch/, /ks/ (written as "x") sounds pronounce "es" as /iz/

Have students practice the following words:

/ s /	/z/	/iz/
books	chairs	dresses
lamps	pens	glasses
students	windows	businesses
desks	schools	dishes
maps	pictures	boxes
streets	cars	houses
plants	numbers	churches
sports	doors	watches
immigrants	rooms	classes
shops	pencils	busses

3 • On a subsequent day, teach the formation of the plural of words that end in "y": change the "y" to "i" and add "es."
Examples:

party-parties	fly-flies
country-countries	cherry-cherries
dictionary-dictionaries	family-families
baby-babies	body-bodies

Note the exceptions: day - days, toy - toys, boy - boys.

3

2 Opposites

Directions *Write two words that are opposites below each picture.*

bad	cold	down	full	heavy	left	old	short	thick	wrong
big	empty	fat	good	hot	light	right	small	thin	young
cheap	expensive	first	happy	last	long	sad	tall	up	

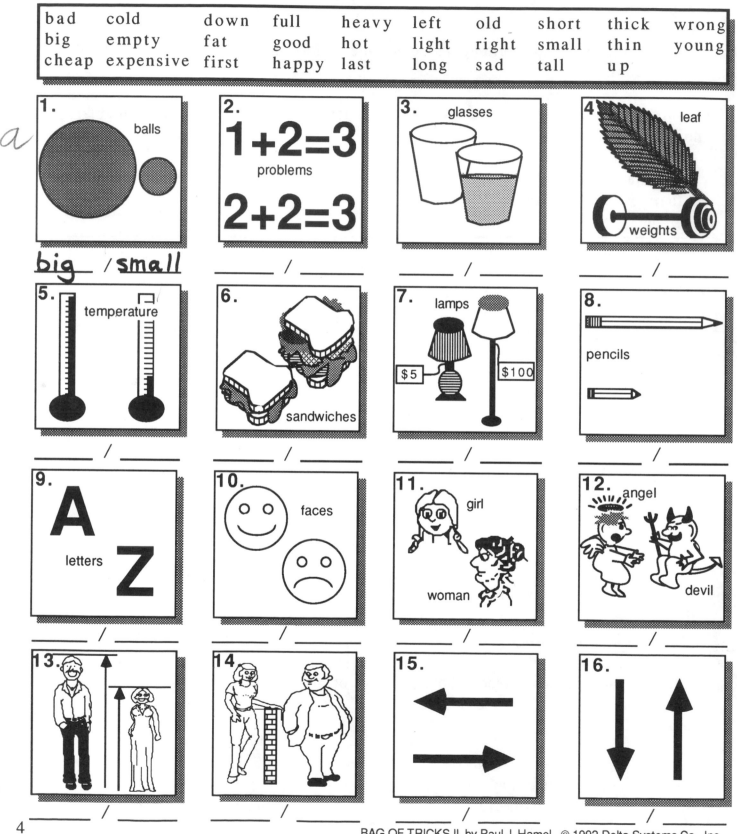

1. balls — big / small

2. problems — ___ / ___

3. glasses — ___ / ___

4. leaf / weights — ___ / ___

5. temperature — ___ / ___

6. sandwiches — ___ / ___

7. lamps $5 $100 — ___ / ___

8. pencils — ___ / ___

9. letters A Z — ___ / ___

10. faces — ___ / ___

11. girl / woman — ___ / ___

12. angel / devil — ___ / ___

13. ___ / ___

14. ___ / ___

15. ___ / ___

16. ___ / ___

- Review the vocabulary below:

balls	leaf	sandwiches	letters	woman
problems (math)	weights	lamps	faces	angel
glasses	temperature	pencils	girl	devil

- Teach the opposites below:

bad/good	empty/full	happy/sad	old/young
big/small	down/up	heavy/light	short/tall
cheap/expensive	fat/thin	left/right	thick/thin
cold/hot	first/last	long/short	right/wrong

- Practice the new vocabulary by having the students use this pattern:

The first _____ is _____ and the second is _____.
     (item)   (adjective)   (adjective)

Example: " The first ball is big and the second is small."

- Continue practicing the vocabulary by teaching the use of "mean"
  using the pattern:

Student #1: What does " (opposite) " mean?
Student #2: It means "not (opposite)."

Example: What does "thick" mean?
It means "not thin."

- Distribute the handout and have the students write the correct words under the
  pictures. Answers:

1. big/small	5. hot/cold	9. first/last	13. tall/short
2. right/wrong	6. thin/thick	10. happy/sad	14. thin/fat
3. empty/full	7. cheap/expensive	11. young/old	15. left/right
4. light/heavy	8. long/short	12. good/bad	16. down/up

- As a follow-up activity, teach additional opposites:

smooth/rough	sharp/dull	all/none	no/yes	below/above	day/night
narrow/wide	to/from	many/few	high/low	light/dark	new/old
on/off	in/out	more/less	near/far	hard/soft	much/little

3 Imperative

① READ

Dear Joey,   Saturday

Don't forget your chores.
Make your bed.
Hang up your clothes.
Water the plants.
Take out the garbage.
Do the breakfast dishes, and mail
the letters on the table.

Do you have a baseball game today?
I don't remember.
Close the windows, put the dog
outside, turn off the radio, and
lock the door. Be home for dinner.
Have fun.

                    Love,

Joey

② COPY *Organize Joey's chores.*

First, _____   Sixth, _____

Second, _____   Seventh, _____

Third, _____   Eighth, _____

Fourth, _____   Ninth, _____

Fifth, _____   Tenth, _____

③ WRITE *Write some of your household chores.*

_____   _____

_____   _____

_____   _____

_____   _____

     BAG OF TRICKS II by Paul J. Hamel, © 1992 Delta Systems Co., Inc.

1 Before you present this lesson, students should already be familiar with ordinal numbers and the following nouns and verbs:

Nouns: chores, clothes, garbage, bills, baseball game, fun
Verbs: hang up, take out, mail, remember, turn off, lock

2 Before starting the reading passage, introduce the vocabulary and grammatical structures that students do not know. For effective visual reinforcement, use the chalkboard, flash cards, objects, and pictures. Give as many contextual examples or new words as possible.

Before distributing the handout, read the text twice as a listening comprehension exercise, then ask questions to test general understanding.

3 Next, distribute the lesson and read the text again. Have students underline any unfamiliar words. Discuss the vocabulary and expressions the students have questions about.

4 Ask some "True" or "False" inference questions to check understanding.

> **Examples:** It's the weekend.
> The baseball game is today.
> Mother is at home.
> It's Saturday morining.
> The windows are open.

5 Do a read-and-look-up exercise: have students read a sentence silently, then try to repeat as much of the sentence as they can without looking at the text.

6 Tell the students to organize Joey's chores by writing them in the appropriate lines in the COPY exercise. As a class discussion, talk about the order in which the chores should be done.

7 Have students write some of their own household chores in the WRITE exercise. Have volunteers write a list of chores on the chalkboard. Correct spelling and have students copy the list on the reverse side of their handout.

8 **Follow-Up**

• On a subsequent day, give a dictation based on part of the text.

• Use correction fluid to prepare a handout of the text with some of the vocabulary items missing. Have students supply the missing words.

4 To Be: Short Answers

READ *Practice the dialog.*

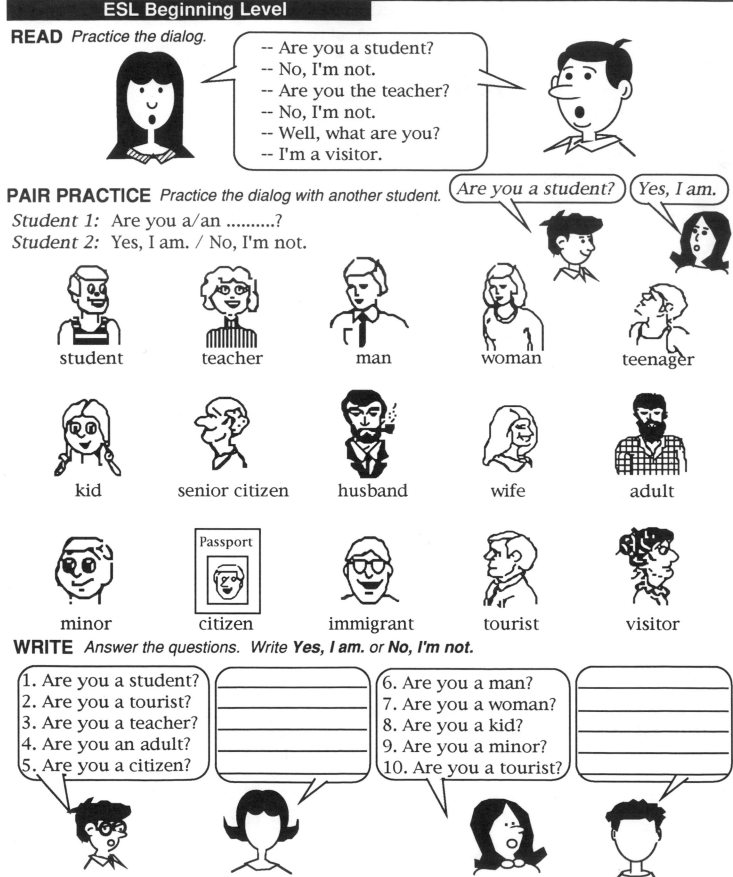

-- Are you a student?
-- No, I'm not.
-- Are you the teacher?
-- No, I'm not.
-- Well, what are you?
-- I'm a visitor.

PAIR PRACTICE *Practice the dialog with another student.*

Student 1: Are you a/an ....?
Student 2: Yes, I am. / No, I'm not.

Are you a student?   Yes, I am.

student   teacher   man   woman   teenager

kid   senior citizen   husband   wife   adult

minor   Passport citizen   immigrant   tourist   visitor

WRITE *Answer the questions. Write **Yes, I am.** or **No, I'm not.***

1. Are you a student?
2. Are you a tourist?
3. Are you a teacher?
4. Are you an adult?
5. Are you a citizen?

6. Are you a man?
7. Are you a woman?
8. Are you a kid?
9. Are you a minor?
10. Are you a tourist?

8

- Review the new vocabulary:

student	woman	senior citizen	adult	immigrant
teacher	teenager	husband	minor	tourist
man	kid	wife	citizen	visitor

- Practice the short dialog at the top of the page with the whole class.

- Do the PAIR PRACTICE exercise as an oral drill. Be sure that the students are familiar with the vocabulary and structures presented in the dialog before doing the drill. (Be careful to correct the use of the articles "a" or "an.")

- Have the students stand up, walk around the room, and ask other students "Are you a/an ....?"

- Explain how to fill in the answers to the questions in the WRITE exercise at the bottom of the page. Read the directions and do a few examples with the whole class.

- Correct the sentences. You may want to project a copy of the handout that has been transferred to an overhead transparency directly onto a chalkbord where students can write and see the correct answers.

- As a follow-up exercise, repeat the exercise substituting the vocabulary below:

Professions

cashier	accountant	draftser	apartment manager
nurse	truck driver	police officer	electrician
telephone operator	salesperson	student	plumber

Adjectives

single	strong	honest	cold
married	friendly	hungry	warm
widowed	smart	thirsty	healthy

Phrases

in the class	at home	near the window
from Europe	at school	near the door
from Mexico	at work	at your desk

- Repeat the PAIR PRACTICE and have students answer with "Yes, we are." or "No, we aren't."

5 Household Chores

1 *Read the list of household chores.*

Chores

- replace a light bulb
- fix the clock
- hang a picture
- water the plants
- clean the bathroom
- wash the windows
- sweep the hallway
- wax the floor

- change the sheets
- wash and dry the clothes
- iron the clothes
- fold the clothes
- dust the furniture
- empty the garbage
- shake the carpets
- vacuum the drapes

2 *Help Nancy and Ron share the work. Write their chores below. Compare your answers with other students. Explain and give reasons for your answers.*

3 **Pair Practice:** *Practice asking and answering the following question with "does."*

| Example |

Student 1: What <u>does</u> Nancy do?

Student 2: She water<u>s</u> the plants.

4 *Make a list of YOUR household chores on the back of this sheet.*

 BAG OF TRICKS II by Paul J. Hamel, © 1992 Delta Systems Co., Inc.

1 Read and explain the new vocabulary:

replace	wash	iron	vacuum	bathroom	clothes
fix	sweep	fold	light bulb	window	furniture
hang	wax	dust	clock	hallway	garbage
water	change	empty	picture	floor	carpets
clean	dry	shake	plants	sheets	drapes

You may want to collect some magazine or newspaper pictures that illustrate the words in the lesson. Paste the pictures on construction paper. On the reverse side of the picture, write the name of the object or action. Use the cards as visual cues in drilling.

Help the students associate the verbs with the nouns in the lesson by drilling. Say a noun and the student must supply an appropriate verb or vice versa.

2 Ask the students to divide the household chores between Nancy and Ron. Have them write the phrases on the handout.

3 As a pair-practice exercise, have students practice asking and answering questions using "does" and the "s" ending of the third person singular of the verbs.

4 Discuss what kind of household duties are done by men and women in this country and in the countries of your students.

5 Have students make a list of their household chores on the back of the handout. Compare students' chores.

6 As a follow-up exercise, you may want to teach expressions beginning with "do."

Expression with "do"		Meaning
do the housework	=	work in the house
do the dishes	=	wash the dishes
do the cooking	=	cook
do the work	=	work
do a good job	=	work well
do the laundry	=	wash and dry cothes
do the ironing	=	iron the clothes
do the bathroom	=	clean the bathroom
do the shopping	=	shop for food
do the cleaning	=	clean the house
do the dusting	=	dust the furniture
do the vacuuming	=	vacuum the carpets and floors
do the gardening	=	work in the yard
do the windows	=	clean the windows
do nothing	=	do no work

11

6 Parts of the Day

Exercise 1 *Complete the sentences with the expressions in the box below.*

in the morning	in the afternoon	in the evening	at night

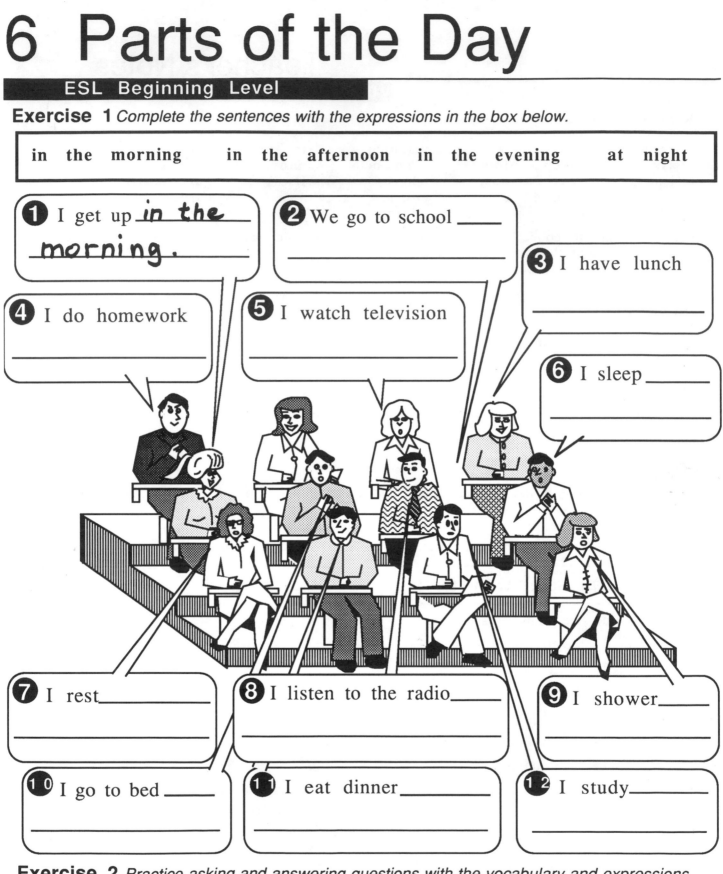

1 I get up *in the morning.*

2 We go to school ____

3 I have lunch ____

4 I do homework ____

5 I watch television ____

6 I sleep ____

7 I rest ____

8 I listen to the radio ____

9 I shower ____

10 I go to bed ____

11 I eat dinner ____

12 I study ____

Exercise 2 *Practice asking and answering questions with the vocabulary and expressions above.*

Student 1: *When do you.............?*
Student 2: *I ....*

12

1 Review all new vocabulary and phrases before distributing the handout:

get up	watch television	shower
go to school	sleep	go to bed
have lunch	rest	eat dinner
do homework	listen to the radio	study

2 Teach the expressions of time in the box at the top of the handout.

in the morning	in the evening
in the afternoon	at night

3 Drill the vocabulary and time expressions by asking Yes/No Questions:

Example: Student 1:   Do you.....(go to school)......in the morning?
                Student 2:   Yes, I do.   or   No, I don't.

4 Practice asking and answering question using "When."

Example: Student 1: When do you......(get up)......?
              Student 2: I get up ....(in the morning)..... .

5 Have students do Exercise 1. Do a few examples with them.

6 Correct the sentences. You may want to project a copy of the handout that has been transfered to an overhead transparency directly onto the chalkboard where students can write the correct answers.

7 Read the directions for Exercise 2 with the students. Have students practice in pairs.

8 **Follow-Up**

• On a subsequent day, dictate sentences with the vocabulary and expressions.

• Teach the expression "at .... o'clock." Drill the word order.
    Example: I get up <u>at 6 o'clock</u> <u>in the morning</u>.

• Teach the variations in the abbreviation of ante meridian and post meridian: a.m., p.m., AM, PM.

7 Days of the Month

Directions *Complete the sentences with the words in the box below.*

Days		Months		
Monday	Friday	January	May	September
Tuesday	Saturday	February	June	October
Wednesday	Sunday	March	July	November
Thursday		April	August	December

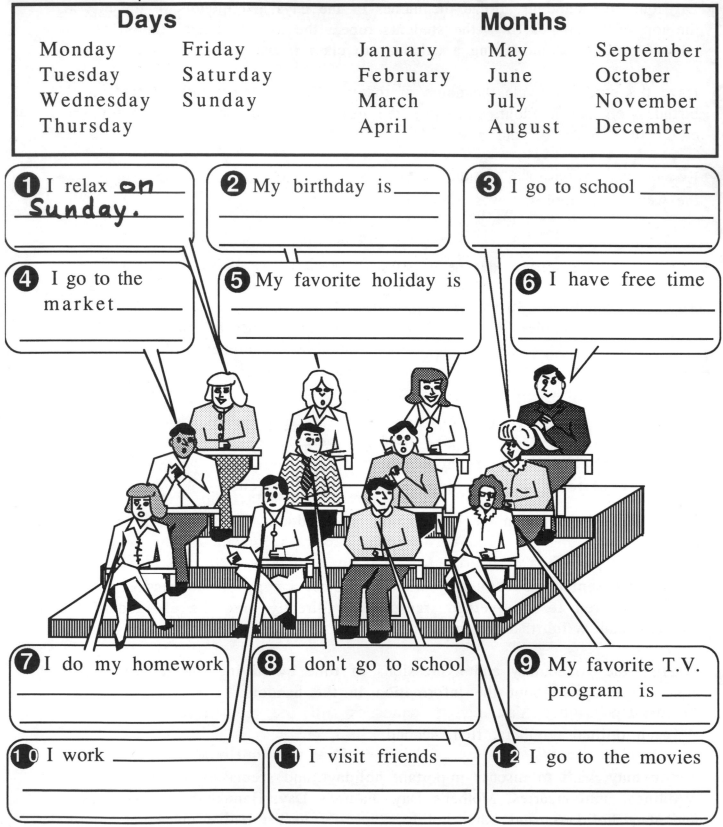

❶ I relax **on** Sunday.

❷ My birthday is _____ _____

❸ I go to school _____

❹ I go to the market_____ _____

❺ My favorite holiday is _____

❻ I have free time _____

❼ I do my homework _____

❽ I don't go to school _____

❾ My favorite T.V. program is _____

❿ I work _____ _____

⓫ I visit friends_____

⓬ I go to the movies _____

14

BAG OF TRICKS II by Paul J. Hamel, © 1992 Delta Systems Co., Inc.

1 Distribute the handout. Read the names of the days and months in the box at the top of the page. Have the students repeat the names several times for correct pronunciation. (Bring a calendar to class if possible.)

2 Have the students circle the name of today's day and the month of their birthday on the handout. Practice the questions "What day is today/tomorrow/ etc.?" and "When is your birthday?"

3 Explain that we use "in" with months and years, and "on" for dates and days of the week. Examples: I was born in November.

I was born in 1945.

I was born on November 29th.

I was born on November 29, 1945.

You may want to present variations for dates.

Examples: I was born on the twenty-ninth of November.

I was born on Thursday, November 29th.

4 Review the phrases and words below:

relax	holiday	program
birthday	free time	work
market	homework	visit
favorite	don't	friends

5 Have the students fill in the balloons on the handout. Do a few examples with them.

6 Correct the sentences. You may want to project a copy of the handout that has been transfered to an overhed transparency directly onto the chalkboard where students can write the correct answers.

7 Practice the vocabulary and expressions of time by having the students ask and answer questions about the information in the handout.

8 Follow-Up

• Teach ordinal numbers: first, second, third, etc.

• You may want to discuss important holidays and special occasions such as weddings, anniversaries, Mother's Day, Father's Day, Hanukkah, Easter, local and state holidays, and other holidays specific to the native or resident country of the students.

8 In, On, At

1 *Read the addresses on the envelopes.*

Miss Susan Babcock
1234 Almaden Rd.
San Jose, CA 95008

Ms. Doris Wilson
943 N. Curson Ave. #4
Pasadena, CA 91106

Mrs. Ann Long
2347 Sunset Ct.
Middletown, N.Y. 10203

Dr. David Uroff
3045 Main Blvd. Suite 303
Chicago, Ill. 80321

Mr. James Smith
496 Maple Dr. Apt. 6
Toronto, Ontario, Canada
M6H3E3

Modern Office Furniture Co.
P.O. Box 150
Los Angeles, CA 90046

City, State, Country	Room, Apt. Suite	Street	Address
in Los Angeles	in Room 123	on Maple Drive	at 110 Clark Street
in California	in Apartment 4	on Main Boulevard	at 2347 Sunset Court
in Canada	in Suite 303	on Almaden Road	at P.O. Box 150

2 *Fill in the sentences with "in," "on," or "at."*

1. Mr. James Smith lives **at** 496 Maple Drive.
2. Ms. Doris Wilson's apartment is _____ North Curson Avenue.
3. The Modern Office Furniture Company is _____ Los Angeles.
4. Miss Susan Babcock's home is _____ Almaden Road.
5. Dr. David Uroff's office is _____ 3045 Main Boulevard.
6. Mrs. Ann Long lives _____ Sunset Court _____ Middletown.
7. Miss Babcock lives _____ 1234 Almaden Road _____ San Jose.
8. Mr. Smith lives _____ Maple Drive _____ Toronto.
9. The Furniture Company is _____ P.O. Box 150 _____ Los Angeles.
10. The City of Toronto is _____ Canada.

Abbreviations

Apt.	apartment
#	number
St.	street
Ave.	avenue
Blvd.	boulevard
Ct.	court
Dr.	drive
Rd.	road
P.O.	post office
N.	north
S.	south
E.	east
W.	west
Co.	company
CA	California
N.Y.	New York
Ill.	Illinois

3 *Practice the following kind of questions and answers about the letters.*

What city does .... live in?
What street does .... live on?
What address does .... live at?
What apartment does .... live in?

He/She lives in ....
He/She lives on ....
He/She lives at ....
He/She lives in ....

BAG OF TRICKS II by Paul J. Hamel, © 1992 Delta Systems Co., Inc.

1 Read the addresses on the letters. Have the students repeat them. Also explain the abbreviations.

- Show that addresses are normally written in the following order:

  Line 1: person or name of company
  Line 2: street number, street name, apartment number
  Line 3: city, state or province, zip or postal code

- Refer to the boxes below the envelopes. Explain that "in" is used with cities, states, provinces, and countries; "on" with streets; and "at" with addresses.

2 Have students complete the fill-in exercise in writing.

Answers: 1. at 3. in 5. at 7. at 9. at, in
         2. on 4. on 6. on, in 8. in 10. in

3 Practice asking and answering questions about the letters. Use questions in which the prepositions are placed at the end of the question:

  What city does .... live in?
  What street does .... live on?
  What address does .... live at?
  What apartment does .... live in?

- You may also want to drill the following variations:

  In which city does .... live?
  On what street does .... live?
  At what address does .... live?
  In what apartment does .... live?

- Note that the placement of the preposition at the beginning of the question tends to reflect more formal usage.

- Point out the written examples of questions at the bottom of the handout. Have students ask one another questions about the addresses on the envelopes.

- Have students ask one another personalized questions such as "What street do you live on?"

4 Follow-up:

- Make students aware of the current and international postal rates.

- Have students bring a postcard or envelope to school. Have them prepare a message, and then address and mail the card or letter.

17

1 *Read the items in the newspaper food advertisement below.*

The Corner Store

SHAMPOO 8 oz. btl.	2.89		**POTATOES** 5 lb. bag	.99
DETERGENT 98 oz. container	5.99		**CHICKEN** Fresh Roasting per lb.	1.29
DEODORANT 2/1.2 oz. btl.	2.99		**YOGURT** 8 oz. container	.65
COFFEE 1 lb. can	2.69		**TUNA** 6 oz. can	.69
ORANGE JUICE Frozen 12 oz. can	.59		**PAPER TOWELS** Assorted rolls	.69
EGGS 1 dozen ctn.	.79		**VITAMINS** Multi-vitamins 100 tabs.	8.29
CHEESE 13 oz. pkg.	2.25		**LETTUCE** Bunch	.49
APPLES 3 lb. bag	1.49		**FLOUR** 10 lb. sack	1.38

Abbreviations	lb. = pound	btl. = bottle
	oz. = ounce	pkg. = package
	ctn. = carton	tab. = tablet

2 *Talk with a student. Use the ad above.*

Student 1: How much does one .... cost?

Student 2: One............ costs ....

How much does one bottle of shampoo cost?

One bottle of shampoo costs $2.89.

3 *Talk with a student. Calculate the correct prices.*

Student 1: How much do two .... cost?

Student 2: Two .... cost ....

How much do two bottles of shampoo cost?

Two bottles of shampoo cost $5.78.

1 • Before distributing the handout, practice reading numbers and prices. Explain that a price such as $2.89 can be re cents" or "two eighty-nine."

• Distribute the handout. Read and explain the items in the newspaper food ad, their sizes, and the abbreviations. (See box below the ad on the handout.)

• Have students practice making sentences modeled on the structure below.
   A/an [quantity] of [item] costs [price].
Examples:
An eight ounce bottle of shampoo costs two dollars and eighty-nine cents.
A ninety-eight ounce container of detergent costs five dollars and ninety-nine cents.

• Repeat the exercise above using the abbreviated form for reading prices.

Examples: An eight ounce bottle of shampoo costs two eighty-nine.
            A ninety-eight ounce container of detergent costs five ninety-nine.

2 • Explain and practice the present tense ("do," "does," and the suffix "s" at the end of the verb in the third person singular). Then practice the questions shown in the pair practice exercises at the bottom of the handout. (Note that students are required to do simple addition.)

• With the help of a student, demonstrate how to do the pair practice exercise using the newspaper food ad. Then have the students continue by working in pairs.

3 • As a follow-up exercise write the following on the chalkboard:

1. cans:	_____	_____	_____	_____
2. boxes:	_____	_____	_____	_____
3. jars:	_____	_____	_____	_____
4. cartons:	_____	_____	_____	_____
5. bottles:	_____	_____	_____	_____

• Challenge your students to name grocery store items that come in the containers listed. Correct the exercise by having volunteers write the items in the lists on the chalkboard. Practice the pronunciation of the items.

19

10 Future Tense

1 *Read Nancy's itinerary.*

Saturday, June 1
- leave Los Angeles
- fly to Denver
- walk in the mountains

Tuesday, June 4
- fly to Chicago
- visit art museums

Friday, June 7
- fly to Boston
- rent a car
- see historic places

Monday, June 11
- take a bus to New York
- visit the United Nations Building

Sunday, June 16
- sail to Miami
- swim in the ocean
- stay with an old friend

Thursday, June 20
- take a train home
- look at the view
- relax on the train

Tuesday, June 25
- arrive home
- take a taxi home

Wednesday, June 26
- return to work
- bicycle to the office

Nancy will take a trip across the United States.

2 PAIR PRACTICE *Talk with another student. Use Nancy's itinerary above.*

Student 1: Where will Nancy..........?
Student 2: She will ....

Where will Nancy go on June 1st?

She will fly to Denver.

Student 1: When will Nancy..........?
Student 2: She will ....

When will Nancy fly to Chicago?

She will go on Tuesday, June 4th.

Student 1: What will Nancy..........?
Student 2: She will ....

What will Nancy do in Boston?

She will rent a car.

3 *Draw lines from the names of the cities to the correct places on the map. Then indicate your city.*

Chicago

Denver

Los Angeles

Boston

New York

Miami

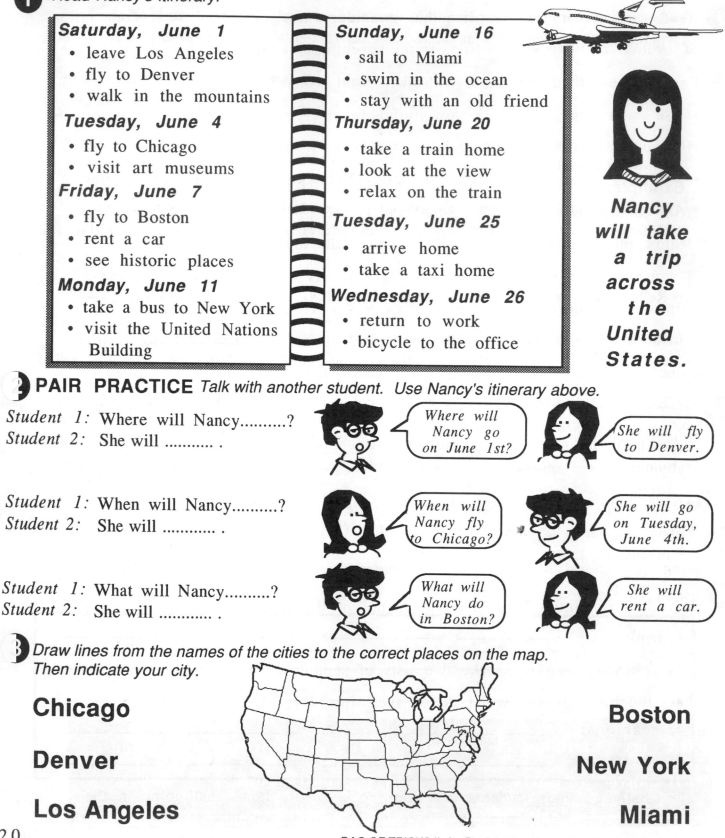

20

1 Read the itinerary and explain the vocabulary. Also review the pronunciation of ordinal numbers (June first, forth, seventh, eleventh, etc.)

2 Explain the use of the future with "will" and won't:"

• Use "will" and "won't" to show future time, especially of plans and promises.

• "Won't" is the contraction of "will not," and "'ll" is the contraction of "will."

• "Will" is a modal. We form the affirmative, question, and negative forms of "will" in the same way as for "can" and "must."

• Show that "won't" is also used to express the idea of refusal such as "I won't eat liver!" Also point out that "will" is followed by the verb and not the infinitive: Contrast "He will drive a car," and "He wants to drive a car."

• In some English speaking countries, "shall" is used instead of "will" with the pronouns "I" and "we." In the United States, the use of "shall" in limited to questions such as "Shall we go?" in which the speaker seeks agreement or concurrence.

• Common time expressions used with the future: later, in a little while, next, two days from now, soon, from now on.

3 With the help of a student, demonstrate how to do the pair practice exercises using the itinerary. Then have the students continue by working in pairs.

4 Have students draws lines from the names of the cities to the correct places on the map.

5 As a follow-up activity, make two lists of sentences on the chalkboard indicating what students will and won't do on their birthday:

On my birthday I will...	On my birthday, I won't...
I'll have a party.	I won't work.

• Have students make an itenerary of their next vacation.

21

Teaching Tip

The following suggestions are only a few of those to be kept in mind when teaching vocabulary.

• Use as many flash cards, objects (realia), and pictures as possible in order to reinforce the words visually. This will help hold interest and aid students in remembering new vocabulary.

• Try eliciting new vocabulary words by means of a sentence in which the last word is not specific. For example, if you want to elicit the word "water," you can say "when I'm thirsty, I drink something. What?" When a student guesses the word, have him or her repeat the original sentence replacing the final word with the specific noun. If nobody can guess the word, say the word and have everybody repeat it in the original sentence. This is a valuable technique because even if the students do not know the word that you are trying to elicit, they are being made aware of the context in which the word in found. It also fosters active listening.

• Define the words and give many contextual examples in sentences, expressions, and situations. Also help define and contrast the new vocabulary with synonyms, antonyms, and homonyms.

• When selecting vocabulary, concentrate on practical, high-frequency, functional vocabulary and expressions.

• Do not overburden your students with too many vocabulary items at any one time. Introduce not more than ten or so new words per lesson.

General   Suggestions

• Create an atmosphere where students are not afraid to make mistakes. Simple communication is more important than speaking perfectly.

• Encourage students to use what they have learned in class in their speech. Encourage them to speak to one another in English during their breaks and free time.

• Be eclectic. Use any method, technique, or combination of methods that work for you and your students.

• Use as much variety in your lessons as possible.

Beginning & Intermediate Levels

11 Word Building

READ

We can form many names of occupations by adding the suffix "-er" to a verb.	Verb		Occupation
	work	→	work**er**
	teach	→	teach**er**
	paint	→	paint**er**

WRITE *Fill in the spaces with names of occupations. Use the suffix "-er."*

1
A computer
programmer
programs   computers.

2
A _____
farms   the   land.

3
A _____
robs   money.

4
A   bus   _____
drives   a   bus.

5
A _____
sings   songs.

6
A   baseball   _____
plays   baseball.

7
A _____
manages   people.

8
A _____
waits   on   tables.

READ

Other suffixes used in occupations:

-ist	-or	-ess	-man or -woman
typist	doctor	stewardess	policeman
artist	director	waitress	salesman
dentist	instructor	actress	policewoman
chemist	actor	hostess	saleswoman

WRITE *How many occupations can you name using the suffixes above?*

_____   _____   _____   _____

_____   _____   _____   _____

_____   _____   _____   _____

_____   _____   _____   _____

WRITE *Walk around the room and make a list of the occupations of your classmates.*

24   BAG OF TRICKS II by Paul J. Hamel, © 1992 Delta Systems Co., Inc.

1 Read the rule and examples in the box at the top of the lesson.

2 Ask the students to identify other words that follow the rule, and write them on the chalkboard. Some words:

manager	builder	programmer	swimmer
reporter	painter	teacher	reader
waiter	writer	driver	speaker
worker	learner	runner	listener

3 Explain how to fill in the words in the WRITE exercise. Read the directions and do a few examples with the whole class.

4 Practice the words in the exercise and from the list on the chalkboard by asking and answering questions such as:

Question: Who programs computers?
Answer: A computer programmer programs computers.

or

A computer programmers does.

5 Read through the other suffixes in the second READ exercise.

6 Next, have the students write as many occupations that they can find using "-ist," "-or," "-ess," "-man," and "-woman."

Discuss the different occupations. Have volunteers write the words on the chalkboard and drill the correct pronunciation of each.

7 Use the last exercise as a group activity. Tell the students to stand up, walk around the room, and ask other students in class for their occupations. Have students write the occupations on the board.

8 As a follow-up activity on a subsequent day, dictate the sentences in the first WRITE exercise as a short quiz.

12 Have to

1 READING *Read the text.*

A counselor is speaking to Bert.

If you want to make money,
you have to get a job.

If you want to get a job,
you have to look for a job.

If you look for a job,
you have to prepare for an
interview.

If you prepare for an interview,
you have to know English.

If you want to know English well,
you have to go to school.

If you go to school,
you have to study.

If you study,
you will make money.

Oh, I see.

2 PAIR PRACTICE *Practice with another student. Use the text above.*

Student 1: What do you
have to do if you ....?
Student 2: I have to ....

What do you have to do if you want to make money?

I have to get a job.

Student 1: What does Bert
have to do if he ....?
Student 2: He has to ....

What does Bert have to do if he wants to get a job?

He has to look for a job.

3 WRITING *Fill out the appointment book.*

APPOINTMENT BOOK

THINGS I HAVE TO DO

Monday_____

_____

Tuesday_____

_____

_____

Wednesday_____

_____

Thursday_____

_____

_____

Friday_____

_____

Saturday_____

_____

_____

Sunday_____

_____

BAG OF TRICKS II by Paul J. Hamel, © 1992 Delta Systems Co., Inc.

1 Explain the use of "have to":
- We use "have to" to show necessity or strong obligation.
- The third person affirmative singular is irregular: "has to."
- "Have to/has to" are followed by the simple form of the verb.
  Example: You have to _get_ a job.

2 Read the text at the top of the page, and explain the vocabulary. Have students underline "have to" as you read the text. Also explain the general impersonal use of the pronoun "you."

3 With the help of a student, demonstrate how to do the pair practice exercises using the text at the top of the page. Then have the students continue by working in pairs.

4 Expand the oral practice by having students practice the phrases below. Have students complete the mini-dialogs in their own words:

(A) Student 1: Why can't you stay?
Student 2: I have to ...

(B) Student 1: Before you leave,
        you have to ...
Student 2: Do I have to?
Student 1: Yes, you do.

(C) Student 1: What's the matter?
Student 2: The ... is broken.
        I have to call a ...

(D) Student 1: Why do I have to ...
Student 2: Because ...

(E) Student 1: Don't you want to ...
Student 2: Of course.
Student 1: Then you have to ...

(F) Student 1: What do I have to
        study to become a ...
Student 2: You have to study ...

(G) Student 1: What's your favorite
        day of the week?
Student 2: Sunday, because I
        don't have to ...

5 Have students fill out the appointment book at the bottom of the handout using sentences with "have to."

Project a copy of the handout on an overhead transparency directly onto the chalkboard, where the students can write their sentences.

6 Repeat the pair practice exercise using the new sentences in the appointment book.

13 Ordering Food

Directions *Fold the page on the dotted line. Look at your side only.*

1 *Listen to your partner's order, and then write it on the order form.*

Paul's Place

ORDER FORM

Quantity	Items

1 *Give your order to your partner.*

Paul's Place

BREAKFAST
Toast with jam, orange juice
Eggs with bacon or ham
Cereal, milk, fresh fruit

LUNCH
Hamburger with French fries
Bacon, lettuce, and tomato
Ham and Swiss cheese
Turkey and sprouts

BEVERAGES
Coffee & tea
Mineral waters
Milk & juices

2 *Now give your order to your partner.*

Paul's Place

DINNER
Baked chicken, mashed potatoes
Fried chicken, fresh vegetables
Roast beef, baked potatoes
Fresh fish, rice

DESSERT
Chocolate layer cake
Ice cream
Apple pie

BEVERAGES
Coffee & tea
Wine & beer

2 *Now listen to your partner's order, and then write it down on the order form.*

Paul's Place

ORDER FORM

Quantity	Items

Fold Here

28

❶ Present and explain the vocabulary on the menus.

❷ • Demonstrate how the students must fold the page in half where indicated.

• Have students find partners. (The first few times, you will probably have to go around the classroom and pair up students.) Encourage the students to pair up with different partners each time.

• Tell them that they must look at only one side of the page.

• One student listens to his/her partner's order from the menu, and the second student writes it down on the order form.

• The students reverse roles for the second exercise.

• While students are doing the exercise, walk around the room, listen to individuals, and correct mistakes.

• When the students have finished, have them check their orders for spelling.

This activity lends itself well to role playing, in which you act as the waiter or waitress and the students respond as customers. Such role playing presents an excellent opportunity to introduce common expressions used in a restaurant:

May I help you?	*Would you like any......?*
Are you ready to order?	*I'd like some .....*
Anything else?	*Could you bring me some ....*
Check, please.	*Do you have any ...... ?*

As a group discussion, talk about where, when, and how much people should tip.

14 Calculating Prices

Beginning & Intermediate Levels

Directions: *Calculate the prices for the items below.*

Coffee .75
8 oz cup
Free Refills

1 How much do two cups cost? $_____

FRESH CORN .25 ea.
20% off with coupon
Regular price
Coupon / Coupon

6 How much do a dozen ears cost with a coupon? $_____

BANANA SPECIAL
2 lbs. / $1.00
Reg. .60/lb.

2 How much do five pounds of bananas cost? $_____

Ice Cream Cone
Half price with coupon, limit one item and one coupon per customer.
.48
COUPON

7 How much do two cones cost with one coupon? $_____

BELL PEPPERS
REG. .49/LB.
3 LB. / $1.00
LIMIT 6 LBS.

3 How many pounds of peppers do you get for two dollars? _____

BUY ONE, GET ONE FREE.
$1.49
Reg. price

8 How many hamburgers can you buy for three dollars? _____

TURKEY
1 FREE 10 LB.
TURKEY WITH
MIN. PURCHASE
OF $100.
Reg. 12.95

4 How much does a turkey cost when you spend $87.05? $_____

STEAKS
Reduced .30/lb.
Were 2.49/lb.
Now 2.19/lb.

9 How much do you save when you buy three pounds of steak? $_____

50% DISCOUNT TODAY ONLY!
Reg. .98 ea.

5 How much do 3 avacados cost? $_____

SALE
Picnic Baskets
$5.69
plus 6% tax.

10 How much is one basket? $_____

30

1 • Before distributing the handout, practice reading numbers and prices. Explain that a price such as $1.49 can be read as "one dollar and forty-nine cents" or "one forty-nine."

• Next, explain and practice doing simple math problems. Use the examples below:

> **Addition:** How much is a .... of .... and a .... of .... ?
>
> **Subtraction:** With a .... cent coupon, how much does a .... of .... cost?
>
> **Multipliction:** How much do eight .... cost?
>
> **Division:** Two .... of .... cost .... cents. How much does one cost?
>
> **Percent:** .... costs .... and 6 % tax. How much is the total cost?
>
> **Discount:** .... is on sale for 20% off. How much does the .... cost?

2 • Distribute the handout. Read the names of the items, the signs, prices, and abbreviations.

Abbreviations		
lb. = pound	min. = minimum	
reg. = regular	ea. = each	
oz. = ounce	+ = plus	

3 • Then have students work as individuals or in pairs to find the answers.

Answers

1. .75
2. $2.60
3. six
4. $12.95; but if the customer spends $12.95 on other merchandise, the turkey will be free.
5. $1.47

6. $2.40
7. .72
8. four
9. .90
10. $6.03

4 • Follow-up: As a group discussion, compare the prices of the items in the exercise and their actual costs today.

15 Too & Enough

READ

> "Enough" means "sufficient" and "satisfying."
> We use it before nouns and after adjectives.
> **Examples:** Jim doesn't have <u>enough money</u> to pay his bills.
> The baby isn't <u>old enough</u> to go to school.

> "Too" means "excessive" and "unacceptable."
> We use it before adjectives.
> **Example:** I can't buy a new car. It's <u>too expensive.</u>

PAIR PRACTICE *Practice asking and answering questions with "enough" and "too."*

1

Why can't Patty
move the T.V.?
(big/small)

2

14 years old

Why can't the
boy drive?
(young/old)

3

Why don't many
people live in the
desert? (hot/cool)

4

Why can't the
neighbors sleep?
(noisy/quiet)

5

$10,000

Why can't most
people buy the ring?
(expensive/cheap)

6

Chicago
125 miles

Why can't Bob
walk to Chicago?
(far/near)

7

Why is Paul
on a diet?
(fat/thin)

8

the   these
they   those
this   them
that   their

Why can't you
pronounce "th"?
(difficult/easy)

WRITE *Write three sentences with "too" or "enough".*

Example: *I am not old enough to retire.*

1. _____

2. _____

3. _____

1 Explain the use of "too" and "enough" by reading the information in the boxes at the top of the handout. Also explain that an infinitive often follows an adjective with "too" or "enough" to show purpose.

Examples: I'm <u>too weak</u> to move the box.
I'm not <u>strong enough</u> to pick it up.

NOTE: Do not use "too" or "enough" instead of "very." "Too" and "enough" imply the idea of a following infinitive.

Examples: He's very strong.
He isn't strong enough to pick up the box.
He's too weak to pick up the box.

2 Review the new vocabulary.

move	drive	desert	neighbors	ring	far	pronounce
big	young	hot	sleep	expensive	near	difficult
small	old	cold	noisy/quiet	cheap	diet	easy

3 Read the directions for the PAIR PRACTICE to the students. Have them practice asking and answering questions.

Example: Student #1: Why can't Patty move the T.V.?
Student #2: She can't move the T.V. because it's too big.

4 Have individual students copy the questions onto the chalkboard. Have other students write the correct answers.

5 Continue drilling the use of "too" and "enough:"

Student #1: Why can't ....work.
Student #2: Because ....

Example: Why can't Boris work?
He's too weak. / He's not strong enough.

Yvonne	Al	Bert	Helen
old/young	sick/healthy	dumb/smart	messy/neat

6 Have the students write three original sentences using "too" or "enough." Read the example at the bottom of the page. Correct the sentences. You may want to project a copy of the handout that has been transferred to an overhead transparency directly onto the chalkboard where students can write their sentences.

16 Dealing with AIDS

Directions: *Read and discuss the story. Then, using the back of this sheet, write an ending to the story. Use the past tense.*

Best of Friends . . .

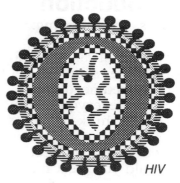

HIV

Jose came to Los Angeles from Puebla, Mexico, and enrolled at Hollywood Community Adult School in the middle of the semester. He wanted to learn more English, and he wanted to make new friends. He made one friend, Eduardo, who was a very friendly and hard-working student.

Jose and Eduardo had a lot in common. Both came from Puebla, both liked the same music, and both wanted to learn English very much. They often studied together before class and many times on the weekend, too.

One night before class, Jose waited outside for Eduardo, who was late from work. While Jose waited, another student in the class, Manuel, walked over to Jose and said, "What's up?"

"Hi, Manuel. Nothing much. I am waiting for Eduardo."

"Eduardo? Listen. There is something you must know about Eduardo."

"What's that?"

"He has AIDS."

"What?"

"Eduardo tiene SIDA. He was in the hospital 2 months ago. Everybody knows. This is why Eduardo has no friends--except you. But if you stay friends with Eduardo, everyone will stay away from you, too."

Jose stood before Manuel and didn't know what to say. Then Manuel turned away and joined a group of students. Eduardo arrived and went to greet his friend, Jose.

"What's up, *amigo?*"

But Jose looked down, his face turned red, and then he left the campus. Eduardo didn't understand. He thought, "What's the matter with Jose? I hope he's O.K." Confused, he went into the classroom and accidentally bumped into Manuel.

"Lo siento mucho, Manuel! I didn't see you."

Manuel looked at Eduardo with hate in his eyes and said, "*Sidoso.* Out of my way!"

Suddenly, Eduardo felt sick. He never missed class, but he decided to go home. On the bus, he sat down, held back tears and said to himself, "Maybe Manuel said something to Jose . . . I wonder."

_____

_____

_____

_____

    BAG OF TRICKS II by Paul J. Hamel, © 1992 Delta Systems Co., Inc.

Introduction

Discuss the following:

- What is AIDS? What do the letters stand for? (Acquired Immune Deficiency Syndrome)
- How does someone get HIV? (Through exposure to body fluids, unprotected sexual intercourse, or shared needles.)
- Should everyone in this country be tested for HIV? Why? or Why not?
- Do you think there has been progress in stopping HIV infection?
- Do you know anyone who has HIV or AIDS?
- How would you feel if you found out that one of your closest friends had HIV or AIDS?
- Would you treat him or her differently? Why or why not?

Language Activities

- Before handing out a copy of the story, read it to the students as a listening comprehension exercise. Then ask simple questions (who, what, where, when) to test the students comprehension.

- Hand out the worksheet and read the story again while the students underline unfamiliar vocabulary. Then explain the vocabulary.

- Discuss the story. Ask the students to say what they would do in this situation. Ask them to describe a conversation between Eduardo and Jose.

- Review how we form the past tense with **-ed** ending, irregular verbs, the negative **didn't**, and the interrogative **did**.

- Review the meaning and pronunciation of the verbs in the past tense in the story:

Regular Verbs		Irregular Verbs	
enrolled	arrived	came	felt
wanted	looked down	made	sat down
studied	turned	said	held back
waited	joined	stood	didn't know
was	bumped	went	didn't understand
walked over	looked at	left	didn't see
turned away	missed	thought	
opened	decided		

- Have the students write an ending to the story using the past tense.

- After correcting the students' papers, choose one of the best. Use it to prepare a handout with some of the words missing as in a cloze exercise. Read the text aloud and have the students fill in the missing words as they read along.

Follow-up

- Request AIDS prevention information from your school administrator or local AIDS agency. Many agencies offer free lectures.

- You may want to refer to the U.S. Government publication "Understanding AIDS" [Publication No. (CDC) HHS-88-8404] ,U.S. Department of Health & Human Services, Public Health Service, Center for Disease Control, P.O. Box 6003, Rockville, MD 20850.

The story was written by Tom Harkin, ESL Instructor, Hollywood Community Adult School, Hollywood, California. Adapted from "Dealing With AIDS," ESL Advanced Level, Bag of Tricks I.

17 May

① READ

- We use the word "may" to ask permission.

Examples: <u>May</u> I come in?   Yes, you <u>may</u>.

<u>May</u> I smoke?   No, you <u>may</u> not smoke in here.

---

② PAIR PRACTICE *Practice asking and answering questions.*

Student 1: *May I ..... ?*
Student 2: *Yes, you may...   or   No, you may not ...*

... come in?
... go out?
... sit down?
... leave the room?

... help you?
... show you the way?
... ask you a question?
... speak to you for a moment?

> May I come in?

> Yes, you may.

WRITE *Write questions using "may" for the situations below.*

1. **May I keep the cat?**

Suzanne wants to keep the cat.

2. _____

Bob wants to help the cashier.

3. _____

The waiter wants to take the customer's order.

4. _____

Herman wants to take your picture.

5. _____

Fred wants to return to his seat.

6. _____

The patient wants to go home.

1 Read and explain the use of "may" in the box at the top of the page.

Explain that "may" is one of many modal verbs. The most common are: can, could, may, might, shall, should, will, would, must, ought to. Modals do not change form, so we cannot add "-s" to the third person singular. We use modals with the simple form of the verb (an infinitive without "to"). The only exception is "ought to." We place modals in front of the subject to form questions.

2 Read and discuss the vocabulary in the items in the Pair Practice exercise. With the help of a student, demonstrate how to do the pair practice exercise using the phrases. Then have the students continue by working in pairs.

As an extension to the Pair Practice exercise, drill asking permission by having students use "may" with the following phrases:

close the window	use your telephone
open the door	borrow a cup of sugar
turn on the light	come with you
close the door	turn in my homework tomorrow
turn off the light	come in
help you	leave now

Examples:

Situation	Request
It is cold in this room.	May I close the window?
It's hot in here.	May I open the door?
It's dark.	May I turn on the light?

3 Explain how to write questions with "may" in the speech balloons on the handout. Correct the answers by having volunteers write them on the chalkboard. Discuss other possible answers.

4 **Follow-Up**

Explain that we use the word "may" when we want to express indecision. It means "maybe," "not sure," "undecided." "May" often has the same meaning as "might."

Example: Today is a nice day. I <u>may</u> go to the park, or I <u>might</u> go to the beach."

Practice by drilling with the question: "What are you going to do ..... ?"

tomorrow	around ... o'clock	on your vacation
tonight	after class	if you win the lottery

Teaching Tip

You may want to use the following techniques to develop effective listening comprehensive skills.

• After introducing key vocabulary words that appear in a reading lesson or dialog, slowly read the text aloud to your students before having them look at the written word.   Then ask general comprehension questions.   As the end of the reading lesson or dialog, read the text again at normal speed.   The students should not be allowed to read along; they should concentrate on listening.

• Give frequent short dictations.

• When doing drills or question-and answer exercises, have students cue one another whenever possible.   This forces them to listen to each other and become accustomed to different accents.

• Have students work in pairs and groups so that they can listen and respond to one another on a more personal level.

• When practicing dialogs or role-playing, occasionally have pairs of students stand back-to-back so that they must understand each other without the aid of non-verbal (visual) cues.

• Invite a guest speaker, the principal, the school nurse, a police officer, etc., to be interviewed in class so that the students can hear other accents and intonations. Before allowing the students to interview the speaker, prime the class by discussing the kinds of questions they will ask.   By practicing the questions beforehand, students will be less embarrassed about asking questions or making mistakes.

• Give students the opportunity to listen to different examples of spoken English through music, games, movies, slide presentations, videos, etc.

Using an Overhead Projector

• Project a copy of the handout that has been transferred to an overhead transparency directly onto a chalkboard where students can write the correct answers to a written exercise.

Intermediate Level

18 Expressions of Time

DIRECTIONS *Practice making and answering questions orally about the information in the calendar. Use the time expressions with the regular past tense.*

yesterday	last week	before...
the day before yesterday	ago	after...

EXAMPLES

1 Question: When did Daniel walk in the park?
Answer: He walked in the park <u>three weeks ago</u>.

2 Question: When did Daniel call his grandparents?
Answer: He called them <u>the day before yesterday</u>.

3 Question: What did Daniel do <u>before</u> his mother's birthday?
Answer: He shopped for a present <u>before</u> his mother's birthday.

4 Question: What happened <u>yesterday</u>?
Answer: It rained <u>yesterday</u>.

Daniel

Daniel's Calendar

FEBRUARY

1 walk in the park	**2** work overtime	**3** shop for birthday present	**4** attend Mom's birthday party	**5** shop for food	**6** cook dinner for friends	**7** clean the apartment
8 rest	**9** watch special T.V. program	**10** start new book	**11** pick up dry cleaning	**12** visit Uncle Bill in hospital	**13** play tennis with Paul	**14** help Dad clean garage
15 visit new museum	**16** HOLIDAY PRESIDENTS' DAY	**17** finish book report	**18** invite Nancy to a movie	**19** wash clothes	**20** attend a concert	**21** wax car
22 relax	**23** rent video	**24** visit parents	**25** exercise at gym	**26** call grand-parents	**27** rain, stay home	**28** TODAY

BAG OF TRICKS II by Paul J. Hamel, © 1992 Delta Systems Co., Inc.

1 Review the use of the past tense. Explain how to add the "-ed" ending to form the past tense of regular verbs in the affirmative only. We do not use the "-ed" ending with verbs in the question and negative forms. We use "did" with the present tense of a verb to signal the question and "did not" or "didn't" with the present tense of the verb to signal the negative.

2 Explain the meaning of the expressions of time: yesterday, the day before yesterday, last week, ago, before, after. Then, explain the meaning of the phrases on the calendar.

After the students are familiar with the new vocabulary, have them do the pair practice exercises. Pairing exercises give the students time, especially in large classes, to practice important speaking skills. Have each student choose a partner. (The first few times, you will probably have to go around the classroom and pair up students.) Encourage the students to pair up with different partners each time. While students are doing the exercise, walk around the room, listen to individuals, and correct mistakes.

3 **Follow-up Activity**

Explain the three different ways we pronounce the "-ed" ending.

- When the verb ends in a voiceless sound (except /t/), "-ed" is pronounced /t/.
- When the verb ends in a voiced sound (except /d/), " ed" is pronounced /d/.
- When the verb ends in a /t/ or /d/ sound, "-ed" is pronounced /id/.

Examples: "-ed" pronounced /t/: worked, washed, cooked, watched
"-ed" pronounced /d/: opened, closed, cleaned, called
"-ed" pronounced /id/: rested, visited, waited, painted

Dictate the following words randomly. Then, have individuals come up to the chalkboard and write the words in the correct catagory depending on the sound of the final "-ed."

Finally, have students ask and answer questions in the past tense using the words below.

/ t /			/ d /			/ i d /		
asked	looked	washed	stayed	closed	listened	decided	rested	visited
danced	practiced	helped	played	opened	lived	ended	started	waited
dressed	thanked	watched	called	learned	loved	needed	painted	wanted
finished	liked	cooked	cleaned	showed	rained			
			returned	arrived	moved			

19 Following Directions

READ *Put the instructions below in the correct order.*

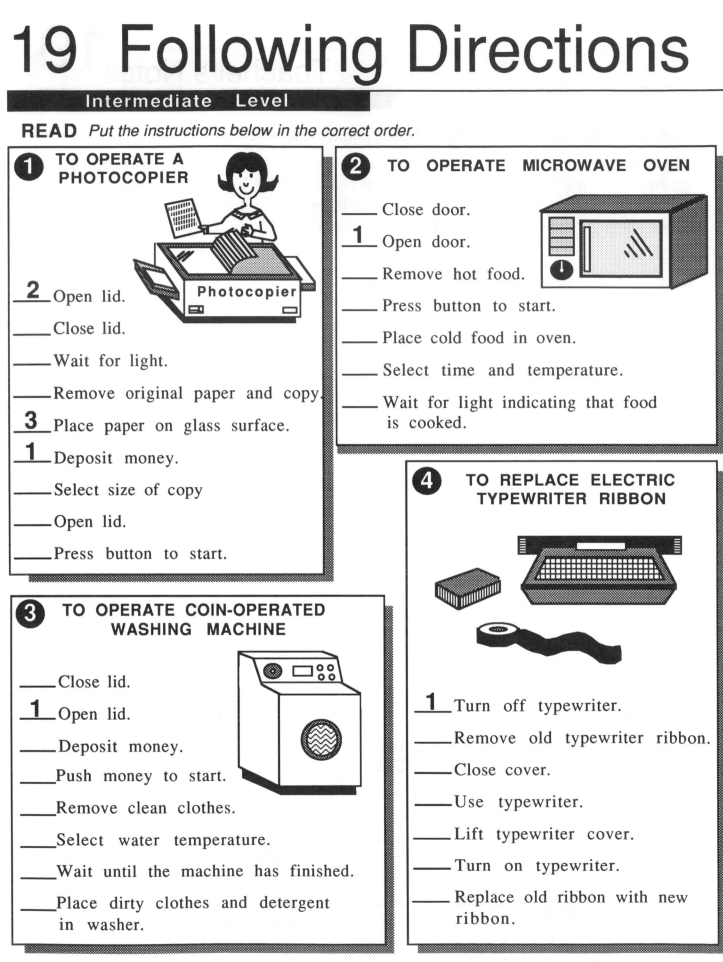

① TO OPERATE A PHOTOCOPIER

2 Open lid.

___ Close lid.

___ Wait for light.

___ Remove original paper and copy.

3 Place paper on glass surface.

1 Deposit money.

___ Select size of copy

___ Open lid.

___ Press button to start.

② TO OPERATE MICROWAVE OVEN

___ Close door.

1 Open door.

___ Remove hot food.

___ Press button to start.

___ Place cold food in oven.

___ Select time and temperature.

___ Wait for light indicating that food is cooked.

④ TO REPLACE ELECTRIC TYPEWRITER RIBBON

1 Turn off typewriter.

___ Remove old typewriter ribbon.

___ Close cover.

___ Use typewriter.

___ Lift typewriter cover.

___ Turn on typewriter.

___ Replace old ribbon with new ribbon.

③ TO OPERATE COIN-OPERATED WASHING MACHINE

___ Close lid.

1 Open lid.

___ Deposit money.

___ Push money to start.

___ Remove clean clothes.

___ Select water temperature.

___ Wait until the machine has finished.

___ Place dirty clothes and detergent in washer.

 BAG OF TRICKS II by Paul J. Hamel, © 1992 Delta Systems Co., Inc.

1 Introduce the vocabulary below before doing the exercise.

deposit	press	use	operate	check	unplug
open	wait	lift	make	adjust	plug in
place	remove	turn on	position	follow	screw
close	push	turn off	tighten	include	unscrew
select	turn	replace	insert	attach	throw away

2 Read through the sentences in the four exercises. Then explain how to put the sentences in the correct order. Do the first example with the whole class. You may want to project the image on the chalkboard using an overhead projector. Correct the exercise by having individuals read the right order aloud.

Answers

Photocopier: 2, 4, 7, 9, 3, 1, 5, 8, 6   Washing Machine: 4, 1, 5, 6, 8, 3, 7, 2
Microwave: 7, 1, 6, 4, 2, 3, 5   Typewriter Ribbon: 1, 3, 5, 7, 2, 6, 4

3 Have students do a pantomime activity. Ask volunteers to act out the instructions without speaking.

• As a review of the present continuous tense, have students act out the instructions using the present continuous. (e.g. "I am depositing the money," "I am opening the lid," etc.)

• Have students practice the past tense by describing what the student did. (e.g. "Mary deposited the money," "She opened the lid," etc.)

4 **Follow-Up Activity**

• For additional practice, place the instruction below out of order on the chalkboard and repeat the activities above.

TO OPERATE A COFFEE MACHINE	**TO REPLACE A LIGHTBULB**	**TO REPLACE A DIRTY FILTER IN A HEATER**
Deposit money.	Turn off the lamp.	Turn off the heater.
Select item.	Unplug the cord.	Remove the heater cover.
Press button to start.	Remove the shade.	Remove the dirty filter
Lift plastic door.	Unscrew the old bulb.	Replace it with the new filter.
Remove cup.	Screw in the new blub.	Close the cover.
	Replace the shade.	Turn on the heater.
	Plug in the cord.	Throw away the dirty filter.
	Turn on the switch.	

43

21 Student Mixer

Directions: Walk around the room and find the students with the information below. Write the students' names on the lines.

1 _____ is the youngest person in the class.

2 _____ has an older brother.

3 _____ is the politest person in the class.

4 _____ has the most brothers and sisters.

5 _____ has the most work experience.

6 _____ gets up the earliest every morning.

7 _____ lives the nearest to school.

8 _____ has the longest hair.

9 _____ has a younger sister.

10 _____ is the best student in the class.

Report Card
Listening   A
Speaking   A
Reading   A
Writing   A

11 _____ speaks the most languages.

Hello!
Bonjour!
Buenos Dias!
Buon Giorno!

12 _____ takes the longest breaks.

Who? Me!

1 Review all the vocabulary and the use of the comparative and superlative.

2 Read the directions at the top of the handout with the students.

• Use this group activity as a "mixer" exercise in which students have to talk to each other to get the necessary information. Have students get up and walk around the room to collect the names of other students who match the description on the handout. Allow at least 15 minutes. This is an excellent way for students to get to know one another especially at the beginning of a new term.

3 Have students practice asking and answering questions about the information collected.

4 Follow-up by having the class make up an additional list of other kinds of personal information (i.e., has a younger brother, older sister, etc.) and repeat the exercise.

5 For additional practice:

• To practice "best", "worse," "more," and "less," have students ask one another personalized questions such as "In your opinion, what's better/worse, stealing or lying?" The following gerunds can be used as nouns in such questions:

watching T.V./reading	*playing/working*	*washing/ironing*
walking/riding	*laughing/crying*	*having a big/small car*
having a big/small family	*giving/receiving a present*	*being happy/sad*

• Have students ask one another personalized questions such as "In your opinion, what's better/worse, winter or summer?" or "What do you like more/less, winter or summer?" List the following topics on the chalkboard:

coffee/tea	*football/cards*	*a movie/a book*
blue/red	*money/happiness*	*daytime/nightime*
dogs/cats	*big/small car*	*long/short hair*
fruit/vegetables	*vanilla/chocolate*	*Italian/Chinese food*
fall/spring	*hot/cold weather*	*classical/modern music*

• Supplementary Vocabulary

of the two	Who's the taller of the two, you or your father?
of all	In your opinion, who's the most famous person of all?
in the world	What's the largest country in the world?
of the year	What's the biggest holiday of the year?
in your life	Who's the most important person in your life?

45

21 Comparative & Superlative

1 *Fill in the spaces below with the comparative or superlative form of the word under the line.*

The United States of America

The United States is a big country, but it is not the **biggest** country in the world.
<u>big</u>

The Soviet Union, Canada, and China are _____ than the U.S.A. The U.S.A. has
<u>big</u>

fifty states. Alaska is the _____ state and Rhode Island is the _____ state.
<u>large</u> <u>small</u>

Rhode Island is _____ and has a _____ population than Alaska. Of
<u>industrial</u> <u>great</u>

all the fifty states, Alaska has the _____ people, and California has the _____
<u>few</u> <u>many</u>

people. Massachusetts and Virginia are the _____ states. Hawaii and Alaska are
<u>old</u>

the _____ states. The United States has many great cities. New York City is the
<u>new</u>

_____. Los Angeles is the second _____ and Chicago is the third. Some
<u>big</u> <u>big</u>

people believe that San Francisco is the _____ city in the country. Other
<u>beautiful</u>

people say that Seattle is the _____ , _____ and _____ city to live in.
<u>clean</u> <u>safe</u> <u>good</u>

The weather is not the same everywhere in the country. The North is generally

_____ than the South, and the West is usually _____ than the East.
<u>cold</u> <u>dry</u>

2 *Draw lines from the names of the states and cities to the correct places on the map.*

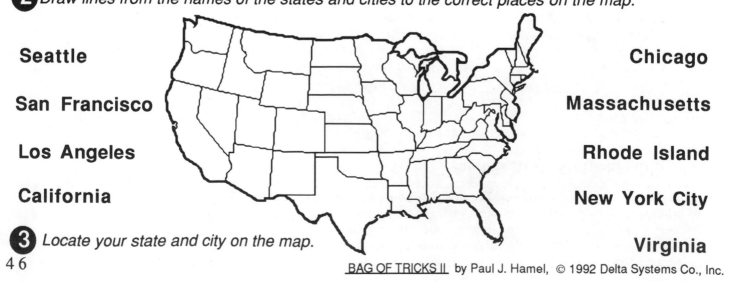

Seattle

San Francisco

Los Angeles

California

Chicago

Massachusetts

Rhode Island

New York City

Virginia

3 *Locate your state and city on the map.*

1 Pose questions about the student's native or adopted country. Ask about the country's biggest city, longest river, highest mountain, largest lake, most beautiful place, most interesting tourist attraction, most important products, and most famous personalities. Encourage students to ask one another similiar questions.

2 Review the uses of the comparative and superlative:

The Comparative
- Use the comparative to compare two objects or people.
- Use the suffix "-er" after short adjectives or adverbs with one or two syllables.
- Use "more" before long adjectives with three or more syllables.
- Always place "than" after the comparative.

Examples: *February has fewer days than January.*
Rhode Island is more industrial than Alaska.

- Some irregular comparative forms are as follows:

good/well ➤ *better than*   *a little* ➤ *less than*
bad ➤ *worse than*   *much/many* ➤ *more than*

The Superlative

- Use the superlative to show the superiority of one item over all others in the same group.
- Use the suffix "-est" after short adjectives or adverbs with one or two syllables.
- Use "most" before long adjectives with three or more syllables.
- Always use "the" before the superlative.

Examples: *Alaska is the biggest state.*
San Francisco is the most beautiful city.

- The irregular superlative forms are as follows:

good/well ➤ *the best*   *a little* ➤ *the least*
bad ➤ *the worst*   *much/many* ➤ *the most*

Spelling Changes
- Most words do not change spelling when we add "-er" and "-est."
  Example: small --- smaller --- smallest
- We change "y" to "i" before we add the suffixes "-er" or "-est" to adjectives or adverbs.
  Example: dry --- drier --- driest
- When a word ends in a consonant-vowel-consonant pattern and the final vowel is stressed, we double the final consonant before adding "-er" or "-est". We never double "w" or "y."
  Example: big --- bigger --- biggest
- If the word ends in "e", only add "-r" or "-st."
  Example: large --- larger --- largest

3 Explain how to fill in the words in the story about the United States. Read the directions and do a few examples with the whole class. Correct the exercise and have volunteers read the text.

Line 1: *biggest*	Line 4: *more industrial,*	Line 7: *newest*	Line 10: *cleanest,*
Line 2 *bigger*	*greater*	*biggest,*	*safest,*
Line 3: *largest,*	Line 5: *fewest, most*	Line 8: *biggest*	*best*
smallest	Line 6: *oldest*	Line 9: *most beautiful*	Line 12: *colder,*
			drier

- Instead of the teacher asking comprehension questions about the text, play a game. Divide the class into two teams. Teams take turns asking difficult questions about the text. If one team asks a question that the second team cannot answer, then it gets a point. If the answer is correct, then no points are given. The team with the most points wins.

4 Have students draw lines from the names of the states and cities to the correct places on the map. As a follow-up activity, have the students find the location in the text on a wall map. 47

22 Some & Any

1 *Read the menu.*

Paul's Place

BREAKFAST

Cereal, milk, fresh fruit
Eggs with bacon or ham
Toast with jam, orange juice

LUNCH

SANDWICHES

Hamburger with French fries
Bacon, lettuce, and tomato
Ham and Swiss cheese
Turkey and sprouts
Tuna salad

DESSERTS

Fresh fruit dish
Apple pie
Chocolate layer cake
Ice cream

SALADS

Leafy green garden salad
Assorted Dressings Available
Ranch, Thousand Island, Blue, French, Light
Pasta salad
Fresh fruit salad

DINNER

Baked chicken, mashed potatoes
Fresh fish, french fried potatoes
Fried chicken, fresh vegetables
Roast beef, baked potatoes
Seafood plate, rice

BEVERAGES

Coffee & tea
Mineral waters
Diet & regular sodas
Wine & beer

---

2 *Talk with a student. Use the menu.*

Student 1: What would you like to order?
Student 2: I'd like some ....

3 *Talk with a student. Use the words below.*

Student 1: Does the restaurant have any ....?
Student 2: Yes, it has some ....?
or
No, it doesn't have any ....

hot dogs	fish	turkey	soft drinks
hamburgers	salad	milk	pastries
omelets	cookies	carrots	roast beef

   BAG OF TRICKS II by Paul J. Hamel, © 1992 Delta Systems Co., Inc.

1 Read the items on the menu and explain the types of food.

2 Explain the use of "some" and "any."
• Use "some" as an indefinite article or pronoun in the affirmative. "Some" can often be omitted. Example: "I'd like some chicken."
• We usually use "any" in questions and in negative sentences. "Any" can often be omitted. Examples: "Does the restaurant have any cookies?" "No, it doesn't have any cookies" or "It doesn't have any."

3 Practice the use of "some" and "any." Gather groups of small items such as paper clips, coins, and buttons, which can be concealed in the palm of the hand. Randomly distribute the items to several students (ideally fifty percent of the class). Make sure that these students have several of each item. Drill the structure by having individual students ask questions of other students. For example:

Student 1:   Do you have any paper clips?
Student 2:   Yes, I have some. (The student has the item.)

Student 3:   Do you have any coins?
Student 4:   No, I have some buttons. (The student has a different item.)

Student 5:   Do you have any buttons?
Student 6:   No, I don't have any. (The student has nothing.)

4 Teach the mini-dialog in the Pair Practice exercises and demonstrate how to do this activity with the help of a student. Then have the students continue the exercise by working in pairs.

5 This activity lends itself well to role playing, in which you act as the waiter or waitress and the students respond as customers. Such role playing presents an excellent opportunity to introduce common expressions used in a restaurant:

May I help you?   *Would you like any......?*
Are you ready to order?   *I'd like some .....*
Anything else?   *Could you bring me some ....*
Check, please.   *Do you have any ...... ?*

6 **Cultural Note**

Depending on the geographical area, the meals of the day are known as either breakfast, lunch, and dinner; or breakfast, dinner, and supper. The word brunch is a combination of the words breakfast and lunch and refers to a late-morning meal especially on the weekend.

Intermediate Level

Directions: How well do you know your classmates? Walk around the room and find the students with the qualities below. Write the students' names on the lines.

1 _____ learns fast.

2 _____ studies seriously.

3 _____ talks to people politely.

4 _____ follows directions correctly.

Direction #1: Read the rules

Direction #2: Write the words

5 _____ works hard.

6 _____ does the homework carefully.

Homework A+

7 _____ drives safely.

8 _____ listens quietly.

Sh!

9 _____ dresses beautifully.

10 _____ speaks clearly.

If you speak English good, you don't speak English well.

11 _____ makes friends easily.

12 _____ teaches well.

50

1 Review all the vocabulary and the use of adverbs of manner. Explain:
- Adverbs of manner usually answer the question "How...?"
- Most adverbs follow the verb.
- Most adverbs are formed by simply adding "-ly." (Examples: quickly, slowly)
- The letter "y" changes to "i" before adding "-ly." (Example: busy-busily)
- When a word ends in "le," drop the "e," and simply add "y." The letter "e" is no longer pronounced. (Example: comfortable - comfortably)
- Do NOT drop the final "l" when adding "-ly." (Example: careful - carefully)
- Unlike most adverbs, "well," "fast," and "hard" are irregular forms and do not end in "-ly."
- Point out that "hard" is also used as an adjective meaning "difficult" as well as the opposite of "soft."
- Do NOT confuse "hard" with "hardly." "Hardly" is an adverb of frequency and is often used with "ever." "Hardly" answers the question "How often...?" It means "almost never."
- "Well" can also be an adjective meaning "healthy."

2 Read the directions at the top of the handout with the students. Use this group activity as a "mixer" exercise in which students have to talk to each other to get the necessary information. Have students get up and walk around the room to collect the names of other students who match the description on the handout. Allow at least 15 minutes. (This is an excellent way for students to get to meet one another, especially at the beginning of a new term.)

3 Have students practice asking and answering questions about the information collected. Ask questions such as "Who ... ?" and How does ... ... ?"

4 Have students ask one another personalized questions such as:

How do you work?   How do you swim/run?
How do you do your homework?   How do you study?
How do you speak?   How do you dance?
How do you play games?   How do you sleep?

5 Follow-up by having the class make up an additional list of other kinds of personal information (e.g., works accurately, listens attentively, runs quickly). Make a handout with the new list and repeat the lesson.

6 As an additional follow-up exercise, you may want to show that "well" can be used with verbs to form compound adjectives such as:

well-mannered person   well-cooked meal
well-educated man   well-prepared speech
well-dressed woman   well-written letter
well-done steak   well-made dress

51

24 Say & Tell

EXERCISE 1 *Describe what the people are saying. Use the verb "say" on the first line and the verb "tell" on the second line. Use the present tense.*

1 Pay attention!

teacher

student

Say: *The teacher is saying, "Pay Attention!"*

Tell: *The teacher is telling the student, "Pay Attention!"*

2 Leave me alone!

Anne   Steve

Say: _____

Tell: _____

3 Take a card.

Alice   Ray

Say: _____

Tell: _____

4 Turn right.

student   dance instructor

Say: _____

Tell: _____

5 Drive carefully.

Tom   Bob

Say: _____

Tell: _____

6 Prepare for take-off.

pilot   crew

Say: _____

Tell: _____

EXERCISE 2 *Repeat the exercise above on another sheet of paper using the simple past tense.*

        Examples: The teacher said, "Pay attention!"
                     The teacher told the student, "Pay attention!"

EXERCISE 3 *Repeat the exercise above using the past tense and an infinitive.*

        Examples: The teacher said to pay attention.
                     The teacher told the student to pay attention.

1 Before distributing the handout explain the use of "say" and "tell."

- The verbs "say" and "tell" have the same meaning, but they are used in different ways.
- They have irregular forms in the past tense: "said" and "told."
- We use "tell" when we "tell somebody something."
- We use "say" when we "say something (to somebody)."
- We also use "tell" in expressions such as "tell a story, a lie, or a joke."

2 Discuss the meanings of the words in the balloons on the handout.

3 • Drill the use of "say" orally using the pictures.
   Example: Student 1: What is the teacher saying?
                   Student 2: The teacher is saying, "Pay attention!"

- Next drill the use of "tell" with the same pictures.
   Example: Student 1: What is the teacher telling the student?
                   Student 2: The teacher is telling the student, "Pay attention!"

4 Do Exercises 2 and 3 orally using the pictures on the handout.

5 Have students write sentences on the handout using "say" and "tell." Then, correct the answers.

Answers

1. The teacher is saying, "Pay attention!"
   The teacher is telling the student, "Pay attention!"

2. Anne is saying, "Leave me alone!"
   Anne is telling, Steve "Leave me alone!"

3. Alice is saying, "Take a card."
   Alice is telling Ray, "Take a card."

4. The dance instructor is saying, "Turn right."
   The dance instructor is telling the student, "Turn right."

5. Tom is saying, "Drive carefully."
   Tom is telling Bob, "Drive carefully."

6. The pilot is saying, "Prepare for take-off."
   The pilot is telling the crew, "Prepare for take-off.

6 Have students do Exercises 2 and 3 in writing for homework.

25 Relative Pronoun: Who

PAIR PRACTICE *Talk with another student. Use the phrases below.*

THE COMPUTER STORE

SALE

CASHIER WANTED

What kind of person is the store owner looking for?

The owner is looking for a person who is honest.

Student **1:** What kind of person is the store owner looking for?
Student **2:** The owner is looking for a person who ....

1
• is honest

2
16 +21 37
• is good with numbers

3
Training Certificate
• has training

4
• can use a computer

5
$ $ $
• handles money well

6
• works well with people

7
• isn't lazy

8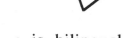
Buenos días!
• is bilingual

WRITE *Write sentences with "who." Describe YOUR qualities. Begin with "I am a person who....."*

Example: *I am a person who likes to work.*

1. _____

2. _____

3. _____

BAG OF TRICKS II by Paul J. Hamel, © 1992 Delta Systems Co., Inc.

1 Explain the use of the relative pronoun "who." Explain that we usually use "who" for people and "that" for things.
Examples:
The owner of the store is looking for a person <u>who</u> is honest.
Jim is looking for a job <u>that</u> is near his home.

2 Review the new vocabulary

honest	use	well
numbers	computer	lazy
training	to handle	bilingual

3 Distribute the handout. Read the directions with the students and do the Pair Practice Drill orally in class.

4 Discuss other qualities that the owner might want in an employee:

reliable	intelligent	polite	accurate
punctual	neat	courteous	lives nearby
friendly	clean	helpful	likes to do a good job
trustworthy	well-groomed	has experience	doesn't argue
knowledgeable	well-dressed	energetic	can make change
listens well	speaks English	learns quickly	can work on weekends

5 Write the words on the chalkboard and repeat the drill using the new words.

6 Have the students write three original sentences using "who." Read the example at the bottom of the page.

7 Correct the sentences. You may want to project a copy of the handout that has been transferred to an overhead transparency directly onto the chalkboard where students can write their sentences.

8 **Follow-Up**

Teach that relative pronouns can be used as the subject or object of a sentence, but when we use them as the object, they can be deleted.
Examples:
The owner is the person who you want to see.
The owner is the person ~~who~~ you want to see.

This is the job that I want.
This is the job ~~that~~ I want.

55

26 Relative Pronoun: That

PAIR PRACTICE *Talk with another student. Use the phrases below.*

EMPLOYMENT OPPORTUNITIES

HELP WANTED	JOB ADS	FULL TIME	PART TIME

What kind of job do you want?

I want a job that pays well.

Student 1: What kind of job do you want?
Student 2: I want a job that ....

1 PAYCHECK $$$
• pays well

2
• is near my home

3 Training Certificate
• gives training

4 Insurance Policy
• has benefits

5
• has good working conditions

6 PROMOTION
• gives me the chance to advance

7 TIME CARD 8 To 5
• has a good schedule

8 Yawn
• isn't boring

WRITE *Write sentences with "that" Describe a job you want. Begin with "I want a job that.........."*

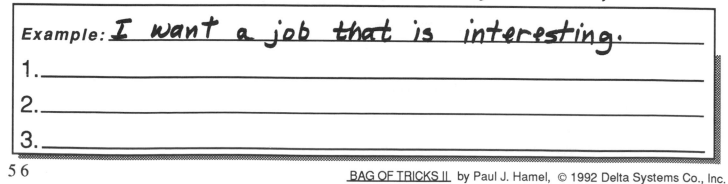

Example: *I want a job that is interesting.*

1. _____

2. _____

3. _____

BAG OF TRICKS II by Paul J. Hamel, © 1992 Delta Systems Co., Inc.

1 Explain the use of the relative pronoun "that." Explain that we usually use "who" for people and "that" for things.
Examples:
There are many people <u>who</u> need work.
Jane is looking for a job <u>that</u> is near her home.

2 Review the new vocabulary

pay	training	benefits	time card
boring	certificate	promotion	schedule
paycheck	insurance policy	working conditions	yawn

3 Distribute the handout. Read the directions with the students and do the Pair Practice Drill orally in class.

4 Discuss other qualities that a person might look for in a job:
- flexible
- enjoyable
- allows you to make decisions
- pays for your education
- pays for mileage
- pays for holidays
- give long vacations
- pays for retirement
- listens to your suggestions
- hires helpful employees

5 Write the new phrases on the chalkboard and repeat the drill using them.

6 Have the students write three original sentences using "that." Read the example at the bottom of the page.

7 Correct the sentences. You may want to project a copy of the handout that has been transferred to an overhead transparency directly onto the chalkboard where students can write their sentences.

8 **Follow-Up**

Teach that relative pronouns can be used as the subject or object of a sentence, but when we use them as the object, they can be deleted.
Examples:
The owner is the person who you want to see.
The owner is the person ~~who~~ you want to see.

This is the job that I want.
This is the job ~~that~~ I want.

27 Could

READ

- We use the word "could" to ask a polite question.

Examples: <u>Could</u> you please help me?   Yes, I <u>could</u>.
<u>Could</u> you tell me the time?   Yes, it's 9 o'clock.

② PAIR PRACTICE *Practice asking and answering questions.*

Student 1: Could you please ..... ?
Student 2: Yes, I could... or No, I couldn't...

... help me?
... tell me the time?
... show me the way out?
... change twenty dollars?

... repeat that?
... come for dinner?
... have lunch with me?
... direct me to the office?

Could you please help me?

Yes, I could.

WRITE *Write questions using "could" for the situations below.*

1. _____

She needs
some information.

2. _____

He doesn't understand so he
asks the teacher to repeat.

3. _____

You need some gas
at a gas station.

4. _____

He wants a cookie.

5. _____

He need directions
to the nearest phone.

6. _____

They want another
bottle of wine.

   <u>BAG OF TRICKS II</u> by Paul J. Hamel, © 1992 Delta Systems Co., Inc.

1 Read and explain the use of "could" in the box at the top of the page.

Explain that "could" is one of many modal verbs. The most common are: can, could, may, might, shall, should, will, would, must, ought to. Modals do not change form, so we cannot add "-s" to the third person singular. We use modals with the simple form of the verb (an infinitive without "to") The only exception is "ought to." We place modals in front of the subject to form questions.

2 Read and discuss the vocabulary in the items in the Pair Practice exercise. With the help of a student, demonstrate how to do the pair practice exercise using the phrases. Then have the students continue by working in pairs.

As an extension to the Pair Practice exercise, drill polite requests by having students use "could" with the following phrases:

pass the butter	lower the volume
give me change for ...	open this jar for me
give me an application	hold (wait on the telephone)
explain this word	tell me how much this costs
wrap this present	do me a favor
fill 'er up (gas for a car)	tell me the time
give me a ride	lend me ...
tell me how I can get to ... (place)	hand me the ...

3 Describe situations in which the students must respond with "Could you...?"

Stimulus	**Response**
The door is open. It's cold.	*Could you please close the door?*
You lost your watch and you don't know the time.	*Could you please tell me the time?*
You are at a restaurant with a friend and you don't have any money.	*Could you lend me some money?*

4 Explain how to write questions with "could" in the speech balloons on the handout. Correct the answers by having volunteers write them on the chalkboard. Discuss other possible answers.

5 **Follow-Up**

• Repeat the pair practice exercise using the expression "Would you please...?"

• Practice using "could" as the past tense of "can." Practice the phrases:
"Could you .... when you came to this country?
"Yes, I could........" or "No, I couldn't........"

28 Should

1 READ

• We use the word "should" when we want to express an opinion or give advice. "Should" is sometimes a polite form of "must."

Examples: You _shouldn't_ smoke. It's bad for you.

You _should_ come to school early to get a good seat.

2 PAIR PRACTICE *Practice asking and answering questions in class.*

Student 1: What should you do ....?
Student 2: You should ....

... to find a job?
... to learn English?
... to learn English well?
... to make friends?

... to keep friends?
... if you see an accident?
... if you are very sick?
... if you can't go to work today?

What should you do to find a job?

You should look in the newspaper.

3 WRITE *What should the people in the pictures do? Write your opinion under each picture.*

I love you.

1. They should get married.

This car doesn't work!

2. _____

Cough! Cough! Cough! Cough!

3. _____

I can't read.

4. _____

How does this computer work?

5. _____

I need money.

6. _____

BAG OF TRICKS II by Paul J. Hamel, © 1992 Delta Systems Co., Inc.

1 Read and explain the use of "should" in the box at the top of the page.

Explain that "should" is a modal verbs.
- "Should" generally has the same meaning as "ought to."
- Other modal verbs are: can, could, may, might, shall, should, will, would, must, ought to.

- Modals do not change form, so we cannot add "-s" to the third person singular. We use modals with the simple form of the verb (an infinitive without "to")

Example: We should come early to get a good seat.

- We place modals in front of the subject to form questions.

Example: Should we go to the beach?

2 Read and discuss the vocabulary in the items in the Pair Practice exercise. With the help of a student, demonstrate how to do the pair practice exercise using the phrases. Then have the students continue by working in pairs.

3 Describe situations in which the students must respond with "should."
Examples:

Stimulus	Response
It's my mother's birthday.	I should get her a present.
Jim smokes too many cigarettes.	Jim should stop smoking.
Pablo can't speak English.	Pablo should go to school.

4 Explain how to write sentences with "should" below the pictures on the handout. Correct the answers by having volunteers write them on the chalkboard. Discuss other possible answers.

5 As a follow-up activity, repeat the pair practice exercise. Contrast "should" and "ought to" using the following rejoinder:

Student 1: What should you do .... ?

Student 2: You ought to .....

29 Might

1 READ
- We use the word "might" when we want to express indecision. It means "maybe," "not sure," "undecided."

Example: Today is a nice day. I <u>might</u> go to the park, or I <u>might</u> go to the beach.

2 PAIR PRACTICE *Practice asking and answering questions in class.*

Student 1: *What are you going to do ... ?*
Student 2: *I don't know. I might ...*

... tonight?   ... later?
... tomorrow?   ... after class today?
... around ... o'clock?   ... on your vacation?
... on the weekend?   ... if you win the lottery?
... on your birthday? ... if you lose your job?

What are you going to do tomorrow?

I don't know. I might go to the beach.

3 WRITE *What should the people in the pictures do? Write your opinion under each picture.*

He's thinking of taking a vacation.

1. *I might go to Florida.*

Will you come to the company picnic?

2. _____

What are you going to order?

3. I don't know. _____

Where will you go on your next vacation?

4. _____

Who will you vote for in the next election?

5. _____

What will he be when he grows up?

6. _____

 BAG OF TRICKS II by Paul J. Hamel, © 1992 Delta Systems Co., Inc.

1 Read and explain the use of "might" in the box at the top of the page.

Explain that "might" is a modal verb.

- "Might" + verb (simple form) expresses possibility in the future or at present.
- "Might" often has the same meaning as "may."
- Other modal verbs are: can, could, may, shall, should, will, would, must, ought to.
- Modals do not change form, so we cannot add "-s" to the third person singular. We use modals with the simple form of the verb (an infinitive without "to").

  Example: We might go to the movies, or we might go to the theater on Saturday.

2 Read and discuss the vocabulary in the items in the Pair Practice exercise. With the help of a student, demonstrate how to do the pair practice exercise using the phrases. Then have the students continue by working in pairs.

Describe situations in which the students must respond with "might."

3 Examples:

Stimulus	Response
What are you going to order for dinner?	I don't know. I might have fish, or I might have chicken.
What will you do on your next vacation?	I don't know. I might go to Hawaii, or I might go to Florida.

4 Explain how to write sentences with "might" below on the lines in the handout. Correct the answers by having volunteers write them on the chalkboard. Discuss other possible answers.

5 As a follow-up activity, repeat the pair practice exercise. Contrast "might" and "may" using the following rejoinder:

Student 1: What will you do .... ?

Student 2: I might ..... or I may....

30 Past Continuous

Intermediate Level

1 *Talk with a student. Practice asking and answering questions using the past continuous.*

Student 1: What was .... doing when the fire started?

Student 2: .... was ....ing ....

> What was Linda doing when the fire started?

> She was making photocopies.

Linda

Bill

The managers

1. make photocopies

2. work in the warehouse

3. have a meeting

Albert

FIRE

The fire started at 2:35 p.m.

Doctor Fuller

4. work on the assembly line

5. work in the laboratory

Simon

Tom and Jim

Jane

6. weld

7. discuss a project

8. talk on the phone

2 *Practice asking and answering "yes" and "no" questions.*

Examples:
- Was Linda making photocopies when the fire started?
  Yes, she was.
- Was Albert working in the warehouse when the fire started?
  No, he wasn't. He was working on the assembly line.

BAG OF TRICKS II by Paul J. Hamel, © 1992 Delta Systems Co., Inc.

• Explain the use of the past continuous tense.

1. Use the past continuous to describe an action that interrupts another action in the past.

2. Use the simple past tense after words like "before," "when," and "after," and the past continuous after "while." Examples:

> They **were fighting** the fire **when** the fire fighters **arrived.**
> Mr. Sam Blazes accidentally set the fire **while he was smoking.**
> I heard about the fire on the radio **while I was driving here.**

3. We also use the past continuous to describe two past actions that were happening at the same time. Example:

> We were evacuating the nearby buildings while the fire fighters **were putting** out the fire.

• Read the directions for the PAIR PRACTICE exercise with the whole class. Do a few examples with the whole class. Then, have students practice in pairs.

• Have students practice short "yes" and "no" questions. See examples at the bottom of the page.

• As a follow-up exercise, have students fill in the blanks of the FIRE REPORT with the simple past or past continuous form of the word under the line.

FIRE REPORT

The fire _____ about 2:35 p.m. at the Pacific Plastics Company in a storeroom at the back of the
        begin

warehouse. Mr. Sam Blazes _____ that he _____ when he accidentally_____ the fire.
                    say   smoke   start

Mr. Joe LaBrincha, an employee at the company, _____ the fire and _____ the fire department
                          see   call

immediately. Then he _____ the fire to the company security guard. When the fire fighters
            report

_____ at 2:55 p.m., some of the employees _____ to put out the fire, and others
   evacuate   try

_____ the nearby buildings. The fire fighters _____ the fire quickly and
   arrive   put out

_____ at 3:15 p.m. There _____ no serious injuries and damage _____ light.
   leave   be   be

After the fire, while the fire investigators _____ the warehouse and storerooms, they noticed that
                     inspect

there _____ no fire extinguishers or safety signs. The fire investigators _____ the company
      be   tell

president that his company _____ ten days to install fire extinguishers and put up safety signs.
                have

Fire Investigator

31 Writing Bulletin Board Notes

DIRECTIONS   *Fold this paper down the middle. Do this exercise with a partner. Each of you will select a side. Tell your partner what messages there are on your bulletin board, and your partner will write them on his or her bulletin board. Then reverse roles. Compare your messages only after you both finish.*

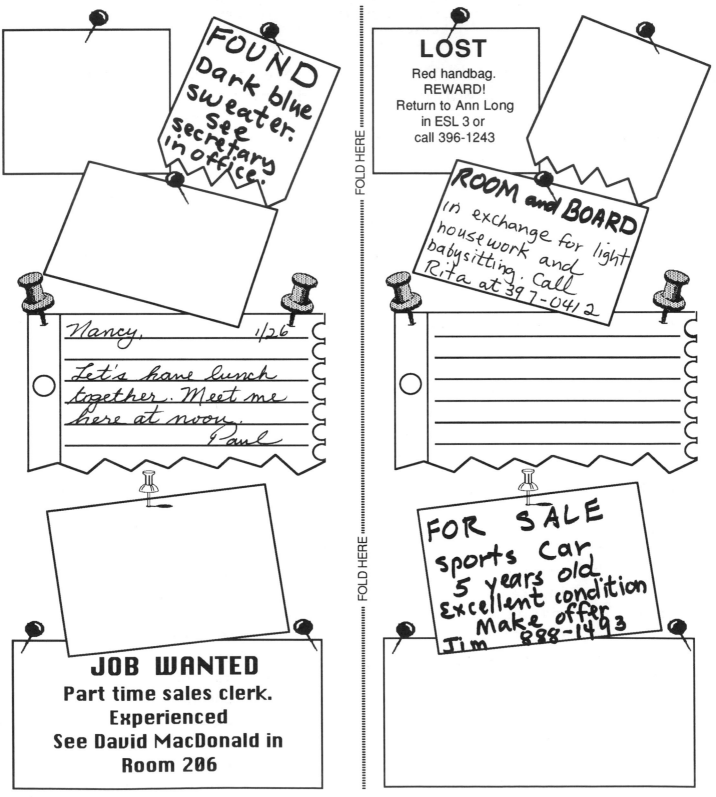

FOUND
Dark blue sweater. See secretary in office.

Nancy,   1/26

Let's have lunch together. Meet me here at noon.
                          Paul

JOB WANTED
Part time sales clerk.
Experienced
See David MacDonald in
Room 206

FOLD HERE

LOST
Red handbag.
REWARD!
Return to Ann Long
in ESL 3 or
call 396-1243

ROOM and BOARD
In exchange for light housework and babysitting. Call Rita at 397-0412

FOR SALE
sports car
5 years old
Excellent condition
Make offer
Jim 888-1493

   BAG OF TRICKS II by Paul J. Hamel, © 1992 Delta Systems Co., Inc.

1 Present and discuss the following vocabulary before students do the exercise.

Found	handbag	excellent condition
Lost	Reward	make offer
Room and Board	in exchange for	part time
For Sale	housework	sales clerk
Job Wanted	babysitting	

2 Distribute the handout and read the directions. Tell the students to fold the paper down the middle. Next, tell them to find a partner. Have each student select a side of the paper. Explain that each student will read the messages on his or her side and that the partner will write the message in the appropriate place on his or her bulletin board. Then they will reverse roles. Have the students compare their messages only after they have both finished the exercise.

3 On a subsequent day dictate the notes as a short quiz.

4 **Follow-up Activities**

* Have students write one another notes modeled on those in the exercise.

* Make a bulletin board in the classroom.

* Develop a one-page class newsletter made up of students' notes.

* Review cursive writing.

* Read the lost and found section of your local newspaper.

* Study common abbreviations used in lost and found classified advertisements:

ext.	=	extension	exp.	=	experienced
eve.	=	evening	gd.	=	good
hr.	=	hour	loc.	=	local
immed.	=	immediate	p.t./f.t.	=	part time/full time
max.	=	maximum	nec.	=	necessary
pri.	=	private	req.	=	required
p.p.	=	private party	@	=	at
nr.	=	near	#	=	number
pd.	=	paid	$	=	dollar
yr.	=	year	%	=	percent
w/	=	with	+	=	plus
info.	=	information	&	=	and
xlnt.	=	excellent	=	=	equal

Teaching Tip

Some Suggestions

• Before reading passage or dialog, introduce the new vocabulary and grammatical structures. For effective visual reinforcement, use the chalkboard, flash cards, and pictures. Give many contextual examples of new words.

• Read the text. The student should not see the text at this point. Use this time as a listening comprehension exercise.

• Ask simple comprehension questions using question words such as "what," "where," "when," and "why."

• Read the text a second time, with the student reading along. As you read, tell the students to underline any unfamiliar vocabulary and expressions.

• Discuss the vocabulary and expressions the students have underlined.

• Ask more detailed comprehension questions.

Other suggestions

• Have students read the reading passage or dialog silently. Then ask basic comprehension questions.

• Have students retell the story in the passage or dialog in their own words.

• After asking detailed comprehension questions, have students ask their own detailed questions of each other.

• On another day, give a short dictation based on part of the text.

• Prepare a handout of the text with some of the vocabulary items missing (cloze-type exercise). Have students supply the missing words.

• Have students write a story modeled on the text or dialog.

• If possible, have students change story from dialog to text or vice versa.

• Do a read-and-look-up exercise. Have students read a sentence silently, then try to repeat as much of the sentence as they can without looking at it.

Advanced
Level

32 Word Building

ACROSS →

1. A .... works in a hospital.
5. Policemen and .... work together.
6. do again
8. not important
11. A banana usually has a .... color.
12. A .... fixes teeth.
13. wash again
14. I don't know how to get to your home. Please give me ....

DOWN ↓↓↓↓

1. A .... drives a car.
2. This road is .... in the winter.
3. opposite of "upward"
4. opposite of "do"
7. paint again
9. .... use typewriters
10. tell again

- Most of the answers for the crossword puzzle contain a prefix or suffix. Listed below are some common prefixes and suffixes.

Prefixes un-   re-

Suffixes -or   -er   -y   -ish
                      -ward   -tion

- Write other words that contain prefixes and suffixes.

Prefixes	Suffixes

- Discuss the meanings of the words above.

70

1 Demonstrate how to do a crossword puzzle. Explain the concept of "down" and "across." Then demonstrate how to fill in the crossword puzzle using clues.

2 Have students fill in the missing words. Do a few examples witht the whole class.

3 Correct the answers by projecting an overhead transparency image directly onto the chalkboard where students can write the answers to the crossword puzzle.

4 As a follow-up exercise, have students list as many words using the prefixes and suffixes in the box to the right of the crossword puzzle. Discuss the meaning of each word.

Answers

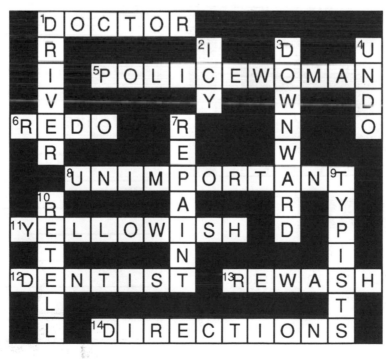

33 Gerunds

1 Practice asking and answering questions about the items below.
Use a gerund after the preposition "for."

Example:

What is a broom used for?

A broom is used for sweeping.

a broom

a lock

a tape measure

an extension cord

a thermostat

a shovel

a hose

a fence

a hand truck

a ladder

a calculator

a flash light

2 Make a list of tools that you use. Then, explain what they are used for.

Tool	Use
1 _hammer_	_A hammer is used for pounding nails._
2 _____	_____
3 _____	_____
4 _____	_____

BAG OF TRICKS II by Paul J. Hamel, © 1992 Delta Systems Co., Inc.

1 Before distributing the handout, explain the use of gerunds:

- A gerund is a form of a verb that ends in -ing.
- We can use gerunds after prepositions in the same way that nouns are used.

Examples
I am responsible	*for*	taking care of the computer.
I am interested	*in*	learning more about computers.
I am thinking	*about*	buying a computer.
I am looking forward	*to*	using my new computer.
I will take advantage	*of*	having a computer.

2 Distribute the handout and review the vocabulary. Practice the mini-dialog and read the directions. Next, show how to do this oral exercise with the help of a student. Practice the activity until the students understand what to do. Then, tell the students to continue the exercise by working in pairs.

3 Extend this activity by having the students think of as many different gerunds as possible for each item on the sheet. List the new vocabulary on the chalkboard.

Examples:
A broom is used for sweeping.
A lock is used for protecting valuables.
A tape measure is used for measuring.
An extension cord is used for connecting a distant electrical item to an outlet.
A thermostat is used for controlling room temperature.
A shovel is used for digging.
A hose is used for watering.
A fence is used for protecting property.
A hand truck is used for moving heavy items.
A ladder is used for climbing.
A calculator is used for adding, subtracting, multiplying, and dividing numbers.
A flash light is used for seeing in the dark.

4 Ask students to think of tools that they use. Have them write the names of the tools on the handout. Then, have them explain what the tools are used for. You may want to make an overhead transparency of the handout that can be projected onto the chalkboard where students can write the list of tools and their uses.

5 As a follow-up activity, practice the following phrases with the students using gerunds:

What do you have experience in?

I have experience in working with computers.

Student 1: What do/are you .... ?
Student 2: I ....

have experience in	responsible for
interested in	waiting for
thinking about	talk about
look forward to	take advantage of
looking forward to	taking advantage of

Directions: *Look at the pictures below as you listen to your teacher's questions. Then, write your answers below each picture.*

1.
Roy Ahuna
Born
8/7/65

Roy was born on August 7, 1965.

2.
Alex & Clara
Married on June 15th

3.
SOLD

4.
GERMANY

5.
Electric Bill
electricity   54.55
by   PAID
by   .56
by   11/29/91
Tax   54.55
          total

6.

7.
Webster's Dictionary

8.

Lost	Found
watch	cat
wallet	ring
dog	coat

9.
DENTIST
613
Main Street

BAG OF TRICKS II by Paul J. Hamel, © 1992 Delta Systems Co., Inc.

1 Explain how the passive voice is formed.

- We for the passive voice by using the verb **to be** in the appropriate tense and the **past participle** of the main verb. (See list below.)

  Examples:

	to be	*Past Participle*	
Roy	*was*	*born*	*in 1965.*
Alex and Clara	*were*	*married*	*in June.*

- Only transitive verbs (verbs that are followed by an object) are used in the passive. We cannot use verbs such as **come** and **happen** in the passive.

2 Distribute the handout and identify items on the page. Read the directions with the students. Before having students write the answers, first do the activity orally.

Ask the following questions.

1. When was Roy born?
2. When were Alex and Clara married?
3. What was sold?
4. Where was the car made?
5. When was the electric bill paid?

6. What was the window broken by? *or* By what was the window broken?
7. Who was the book written by? *or* By whom was the book written?
8. What animals were lost and found?
9. Where is the dentist's office located?

3 Repeat the exercise having the students write the answers below the pictures. Finally, correct the answers. You may want to make an overhead transparency of the handout that can be projected directly onto the chalkboard where students can write their answers.

Answers

1. Roy was born on August 7, 1965.
2. Alex and Clara were married on June 15th.
3. A house was sold.
4. The car was made in Germany.
5. The electric bill was paid on November 29, 1991.

6. The window was broken by a ball.
7. Webster wrote the dictionary.
8. A dog was lost and a cat was found.
9. The dentist's office is located at 613 Main Street.

Some Common Irregular Verbs

Present	Past	Past Participle	Present	Past	Past Participle
bear	bore	born	light	lit	lit
begin	began	begun	lose	lost	lost
buy	bought	bought	make	made	made
do	did	done	pay	paid	paid
drink	drank	drunk	see	saw	seen
eat	ate	eaten	sell	sold	sold
find	found	found	speak	spoke	spoken
forget	forgot	forgotten	spend	spent	spent
freeze	froze	frozen	steal	stole	stolen
get	got	got, gotten	take	took	taken
give	gave	given	teach	taught	taught
hide	hid	hid	tell	told	told
hurt	hurt	hurt	win	won	won
know	knew	known	write	wrote	written

 4 On a subsequent day, use the questions and answers as a short dictation.

35 Passive Voice

Directions *Read the text and fill in the blanks with the correct form of the passive voice.*

Past Tense

Ms. Jensen and a friend thought about opening an ice cream shop last year. They knew that they had to do many things. First, they looked for a good area for the shop. They found an area which **was located** near <u>locate</u> a park. This place _____ because many people _____ there <u>choose</u> <u>find</u> during the weekends. Naturally, many other things _____ : a <u>do</u> loan _____ at the bank; a license _____ <u>take out</u> <u>give</u> by the city government; the building _____; two salespersons <u>inspect</u> _____ ; and finally, some equipment _____. <u>hire</u> <u>buy</u>

Present Tense

Today, everything is going well. Business is good. Ms. Jensen's friend didn't like this kind of business, so she sold her half. Now the business _____ <u>operate</u> by Ms. Jensen alone.

Future Tense

Because business is doing so well, she wants to open a second store. The new store _____ at the beach. She hopes that the new shop will open <u>locate</u> next month. The new store _____ by the assistant manager <u>manage</u> of the first store, and all the new sales persons _____ at the <u>train</u> first store. To save money, the ice cream _____ at the first <u>make</u> store and then it _____ to the new store. <u>transport</u>

Directions *Write sentences in the passive voice with "must."*
What must be done before opening a business?

Example: A location **must be found.**	5. Equipment _____
1. The building_____	6. Ads _____
2. Money_____	7. Bills _____
3. Licenses _____	8. Problems _____
4. Salespersons _____	9. The product_____

   BAG OF TRICKS II by Paul J. Hamel, © 1992 Delta Systems Co., Inc.

1 Explain how the passive voice is formed.

- We form the passive voice by using the verb **to be** in the appropriate tense and the **past participle** of the main verb.

Examples:

	to be	Past Participle	
The shop	is	located	near a park.
The shop	was	inspected	by the city.
The shop	will be	sold	at a future time.

- Only transitive verbs (verbs that are followed by an object) are used in the passive. We cannot use verbs such as **come** and **happen** in the passive.

2 Review the meaning of the verbs in the text and their past participle forms:

Regular Verbs		
Present	**Past**	**Past Participle**
locate	located	located
inspect	inspected	inspected
hire	hired	hired
operate	operated	operated
locate	located	located
manage	managed	managed
train	trained	trained
transport	transported	transported

Irregular Verbs		
Present	**Past**	**Past Participle**
choose	chose	chosen
find	found	found
do	did	done
take out	took out	taken out
give	gave	given
buy	bought	bought
make	made	made

3 Explain how to fill in the words in the text. Read the directions with the students and do a few examples with the whole class.

4 Correct the exercise by having volunteers read parts of the text. You may want to make an overhead transparency of the handout that can be projected directly onto the chalkboard where students can write the answers.

Answers

1. was located	6. was given	11. will be located
2. was chosen	7. was inspected	12. will be managed
3. were found	8. were hired	13. will be trained
4. were done	9. was bought	14. will be made
5. was taken out	10. is operated	15. will be transported

5 Explain how we form the passive voice with modals by placing the **modal** or **auxiliary verb** before **be** and the **past participle**.

Examples *A location **must be located**.*
*The building **must be rented**.*

- Read the direction for the exercise at the bottom of the handout.
- Correct the exercise by having students write their answers on the chalkboard. Answers will vary. Discuss other possible answers.

 6 Do a follow-up activity by substituting the following words with "must" in the exercise:

can	has to	ought to
could	have to	should

36 Passive Voice

① WRITE *Rewrite the newspaper headlines in the passive voice using complete sentences.*

News Daily

12.

Bank Robbed; Thief Caught; Reward Given by City

country. Now is the time for all good men and women to come to the aid of their country. Now is the time for all good men and women to come to the

1 BUILDING DAMAGED, 6 CARS DESTROYED, NOBODY HURT BY RECENT STORM

Now is the time for all good men and women to come to the aid of their country. Now is the time for all good men and women to come to the aid of their country. Now is the time for all good men and women to come to the aid or th... Now is the time for all good men a... come to the aid of their country. Now is the time for all good men and women to come to the aid of their country. Now is the time for all good men and women to come to the aid of their country. Now is the time for all good men and women to come to the aid of their country. Now is the time for all good men and women to come to the aid of their country. Now is the time for all good men and women to come to the aid of their country. Now

1. a bank was robbed, a thief was caught, and a reward was given.

2.

Man Murdered; Suspect Arrested by Police

women to come to the aid of their country. Now is the time for all good men and women to come to the aid of

3.

New Tax Law Passed by Assembly

good men and w... to come to the aid of th... ...ntry. Now is the time ...god men and women to come

4.

Electricity To Be Produced by Solar Company Here

to the aid of their country. Now is the time for all good men and women to come to the aid of their country. Now the time for all good men and women to come to the aid of their

5.

Rare Stamp Sold for $100,000 by Local Company

men and women to come to the aid of their country. Now is the time for all good men and women to come to the aid of their country. Now is the time

Water Pipe Broken; Main St. to Be Closed for Repairs by City

for all good men and women to come to the aid of their country. Now is the time for all good men and women to come to the aid of their country. Now is the time for all good men and women to come to the aid of their country. Now is the time for all good

Famous Painting to Be Bought by City Museum

their country. Now is the time for all good men and women to come to the aid of their country. Now is the time for all good men and women to come

Baby Girl Born in Taxi, Doing O.K.

to the aid of their country. Now is the time for all good men and women to come to the aid of their country. Now is the time for all good men and women to come to the aid of their country. Now is the time for all good

Maria Garcia Named Judge by Governor

their country. Now is the time for all good men and women to come to the aid of their country. Now is the time

Miracle Drug Discovered by Local Doctor

is the time for all good men and women to come to the aid of their country. Now is the time for all good men and women to come to the aid of their country. Now is the time for all good men and women to... ...to the aid of their country.

11.

10.

9.

New Bridge to be Constructed by County

Now is the time for all good men and women to come to the aid of their country. Now is the time for all good men and women come to the aid of their country. No... is the time for all

6.

7.

8.

② WRITE *Rewite the passive sentences above into active sentences using the back of this sheet.*

Example:

Passive: Maria Garcia Named Judge by Governor.
Active: *The governor named Maria Garcia judge.*
Passive: Man Murdered; Suspect Arrested by Police.
Active: *Somebody murdered a man; the police arrested a suspect.*

1 Explain how the passive voice is formed.

- We form the passive voice by using the verb **to be** in the appropriate tense and the **past participle** of the main verb.

		to be	*Past Participle*	
Examples	The bank	*is*	*located*	*near a park.*
	A building	*was*	*damaged*	*by a recent storm.*
	A new bridge	*will be*	*built*	*by the County.*

- Only transitive verbs (verbs that are followed by an object) are used in the passive. We cannot use verbs such as **come** and **happen** in the passive.

- In the passive, the object of an active verb becomes the subject (or agent) of the passive verb. **By** precedes the subject at the end of the sentence.

Examples: **Active:** The governor named Maria Garcia judge.
    Passive: Maria Garcia was named judge **by** the governor.
    Active: We can do the work.
    Passive: The work can be done **by** us.

2 Distribute the handout and use the newspaper headlines as a silent reading activity. Explain that the students must read the headlines by themselves and underline all the words that they do not know. Discuss any new vocabulary. Ask basic comprehension questions to insure understanding.

Read the directions orally with the students. Then, have students rewrite the headlines in complete sentences. Correct the activity. You may want to make an overhead transparency of the handout that can be projected directly onto the chalkboard where students can write the sentences.

Answers
1. A bank was robbed, a thief was caught, and a reward was given.
2. A man was murdered; a suspect was arrested by police.
3. A new tax law was passed by the Assembly.
4. A famous painting will be bought by the City Museum.
5. Electricity will be produced by a solar company here.
6. A rare stamp was sold for $100,000 by a local company.
7. Maria Garcia was named judge by the Governor.
8. A new bridge will be constructed by the County.
9. A baby was born in a taxi; she is doing O.K.
10. A miracle drug was discovered by a local doctor.
11. A water pipe was broken; Main Street will be closed for repairs.
12. One building was damaged, six cars were destroyed, but nobody was hurt bythe recent storm

3 Read the directions for the activity at the bottom of the handout with the students. Have students write active sentences from the passive sentences.

Answers
1. A thief robbed a bank. The police caught the thief. The city gave a reward.
2. Somebody murdered a man. The police arrested a suspect.
3. The Assembly passed a new tax law.
4. The City Museum will buy a famous painting.
5. A solar company here will produce electricity.
6. A local company sold a rare stamp.
7. The Governor named Maria Garcia judge.
8. The County will construct a new bridge.
9. A woman bore a baby girl in a taxi. *(Not commonly used.)* She is doing O.K.
10. A local doctor discovered a miracle drug.
11. Something broke a water pipe. The City will close Main Street for repairs.
12. A recent storm damaged one building and destroyed six cars. The storm didn't hurt anyone.

37 Word Building (Crossword)

Advanced Level

Ten of the words are participles ending in -n or -en.

ACROSS

1. Maureen was determined to open a business, ... she did!

5. The winner was .... a prize.

6. A: Did David open a business?
   B: ...., he didn't.

7. The Constitution was .... in 1789.

8. I am counting ...... getting an "A."

10. All the food was .... before we got to the table.

12. White uniforms are usually .... by nurses.

15. Both English and Spanish are .... in Los Angeles.

16. The winning ticket was .... from the bowl.

Past Participles
ending in -n and -en

DOWN

1. The guests were .... around the house.

2. Bread is baked in an ....

3. Bread .... butter.

4. The senior citizen was .... to the store in her neighbor car.

5. Drugs are .... at a pharmacy.

9. UCLA is a well-.................... university.

11. I am looking forward .... seeing you.

13. Where were you .... ?

14. The abbreviation for "incorporated."

15. A short form for "sister."

80   BAG OF TRICKS II by Paul J. Hamel, © 1992 Delta Systems Co., Inc.

1 Before distributing the handout, point out that many irregular past participles end in -n or -en. List the following examples on the chalkboard.

Present	Past	Past Participle
bear	bore	born
choose	chose	chosen
drive	drove	driven
know	knew	known

Encourage students to think of other words that contain the suffixes -n or -en. Make a list on the chalkboard. Then, ask students to make as many original sentences as possible using the new words. (See box below.)

2 Distribute the handout and demonstrate how to do a crossword puzzle. Explain the concept of "down" and "across." Then, demonstrate how to fill in the puzzle using the clues. Do a few examples with the whole class.

3 Correct the answers by projecting an overhead transparency image directly onto the chalkboard where students can write the answers.

Answers:

	¹S	O				²O		³A
	H		⁴D		⁵G	I	V	E	N
⁶N	O		R		O		E		D
	⁷W	R	I	T	T	E	N		
⁸O	N		V		T			⁹K
			E		¹⁰E	A	¹¹T	E	N
¹²W	O	R	N		N		O		O
						¹³B		O	W
¹⁴I			¹⁵S	P	O	K	E	N
N			I		R			
¹⁶C	H	O	S	E	N			

Common Past Participles Ending in -n or -en.

beaten	lain
begun	ridden
blown	risen
born	run
chosen	seen
drawn	shaken
driven	shown
eaten	spoken
fallen	stolen
flown	sworn
forgotten	taken
forgiven	torn
frozen	thrown
gotten	woken
given	worn
grown	won
hidden	written
known	

Teaching Tip

Expose students through short frequent exercises to writing that is closely related to the vocabulary, structure, and topics you have already taught. Exercises should also be varied, practical, and related to students' daily lives.

Be careful not to overwhelm students. Begin a writing program with simple exercises such as addressing envelopes and writing postcards, notes, and shopping lists. Such initial practice will give students time to learn the most commonly used words which are also the most irregularly spelled, such as pronouns, articles, prepositions, and auxiliary verbs. Once students have learned the basics, gradually build up to longer and more complex exercises.

Suggestions

• Assign writing exercises that reinforce or review previously learned material.

• When giving a writing assignment as homework, reserve the last part of the class period for writing. This will allow you to walk around the classroom to make sure everyone understands the assignment.

• When correcting the students' papers, concentrate on only serious mistakes in structure and spelling. Praise the correct use of recently taught material.

• If you find mistakes that several students are making, note them and teach a special lesson based on these mistakes.

• Include the entire class in the correcting process by copying the incorrect sentences taken from their papers onto the chalkboard, handout, or overhead transparency. Have a class discussion on how best to correct the mistakes.

• Have students rewrite their corrected exercises in a notebook.

• Keep a list of spelling errors to be used in a subsequent dictation.

General Suggestions

• Space our your best lessons and activities throughout the course to keep interest high. Don't empty your entire "bag of tricks" early on.

• Make and collect as many teaching aids (visuals, objects, handouts) as possible. Store them for future use.

Teaching Tip

Do not underestimate the usefulness of dictation. It can be a very effective tool for practicing the four language skills (listening, speaking, reading, writing). It is especially useful as a warm-up exercise at the beginning of the class period to review previously covered materials. Frequent short dictations focusing on commonly used words and expressions used in simple sentences, and stressing function words, such as articles, prepositions, pronouns, and auxilary verbs, will do much to improve students' writing and spelling. Once students become accustomed to the simple dictation, you may want to vary the dictation format to keep interest high. As an example, try the following:

• Dictate six questions.

• After the students have written six questions in their notebooks, ask six volunteers to write the questions on the chalkboard.

• Have six other students read and correct the questions.

• Have six more volunteers go up to the chalkboard and write the answers to the questions.

• Have students read and correct the answers.

• Discuss additional possible answers to the questions.

Other Suggestions

• Dictate the answers, and then have students write the questions.

• Dictate single words that students must use in complete sentences.

• Dictate jumbled sentences that students must put into the correct word order.

• Dictate short cloze (where every sixth word or so is missing) passages. Then have students try to guess the missing words.